I0446713

Etiquette
of the Connected World

Translated by Deepl.com, revised by Debora Dini

Independent Publication
ISBN Code: 9798873508976
Independently published

Introduction

The genesis of this book is closely related to the numerous "on-the-job training" sessions-that is, side-by-side placements between new hires and experienced workers so that training can take place directly "in the field"-that I have organized or conducted over the past several years.

These training events involved an extremely diverse audience, including colleagues from different generations, both digital natives and those less accustomed to technology, people with their first work experience, and employees with many years of work experience but focused on very specific areas.

The trainings were mainly aimed at imparting knowledge on how to interact remotely with customers or suppliers, especially for those operators for whom this was not the main activity, so as to create an additional and supplementary competence in the perspective of Business Process Outsourcing (BPO) services in which interactions with third-party firms or principals are crucial.

In keeping with this, the goal of the book is not to serve as a technical manual. Rather, it is a thoughtful and practical collection of tips and guidelines for effective communication in an online context.

The purpose of these pages is not to teach how to use mail programs or to make you proficient in navigating corporate communication channels, but to create an awareness of the importance of having the right approach to professional digital communications and relationships.

First published on Amazon.it in Italian in December 2023, "Etiquette of the Connected World" allowed me to gather input and insights that led to this revised, but more importantly expanded, second publication.

Netiquette

The Digital Etiquette

The term "Netiquette" is a combination of "net" (both "network" in the narrow sense and short for Internet or network, i.e., network of contacts) and " étiquette " ("etiquette," in the sense of etiquette). This concept began to emerge when early Internet users began to create interpersonal relationships through the net and realized that the same social and behavioral norms that applied to face-to-face communication would have to be adapted to the new "virtual" world.

Just as there are unwritten rules of manners for a dinner party, there is an informal code of behavior online. From childhood, we learn norms of politeness such as "don't talk with your mouth full." However, it is not as common to learn the rules of online behavior, although the basic logic is the same: be courteous to others.

All forms of etiquette are based on interaction with other people, and only the relatively recent and exponentially rapid emergence of online relationships has made it necessary to understand how to apply these dynamics to a remote context as well, through channels never before experienced.

To take one example, no rule of Renaissance etiquette forbade so-called "chain letters" (receiving messages asking for the messages to be sent to additional recipients, creating a "chain" of letters) as the phenomenon was almost nonexistent in the period. Among the few who knew how to write, how many would have spent entire afternoons drafting letters by hand with a nib and inkwell in order to forward a message, unless it was extremely important? And how many days would letters have taken to travel from one city to another?

Typing increased the speed of writing, but the consumption of carbon paper or ink and especially the expense in postage stamps for mailing were still deterrents to the emergence of a Chain of St. Anthony.

With the arrival of photocopiers and especially fax machines in the 20th century came a perception of the potential annoyance such a letter can cause the recipient (and the number of potentially unhelpful communications this creates).

Netiquette

It is only with the advent of e-mail, however, that this phenomenon has exploded to the point where it is necessary to consider whether or not it should be considered rude, in light of the fact that a single user is able to send hundreds of "Chains" with a single click, in a few seconds, at no cost.

This adaptation to the development of relationships--and technology--makes "etiquette" an ever-evolving art and makes Netiquette its latest development--still in constant adjustment as the possibilities for interaction via the Internet change.

One of the best known documents in terms of Netiquette is the "RFC 1855," a "Request For Comments" that provides guidelines for Netiquette in online communications.

The term RFC refers to a set of technical documents used primarily to describe methods, behaviors, research or innovations applicable to the Internet and its related technologies.

Originally started as a way to share ideas among early Internet developers[1] , RFCs have over time become an effective standard for communicating technical specifications and operational guidelines.

---

[1] The first RFC, entitled "Host Software," was written by Steve Crocker in 1969. Crocker was part of the research group working on the ARPANET project, the precursor to what we know today as the Internet. In a sense, then, the RFCs came into being before the Internet itself.

First published in 1995, RFC 1855 contributed significantly to defining the ground rules for online communication. It addressed topics such as formatting e-mail, using appropriate tones in messages, and respecting the privacy of others-topics that previously would not have made sense to talk about.

Relevant in this regard is to quote an excerpt from its introductory section, aimed precisely at explaining why the need for the birth of the document itself was necessary:

"In the past, the population of people using the Internet had 'grown up' with the Internet, were technically minded, and understood the nature of the transport and the protocols.
Today, the community of Internet users includes people who are new to the environment.
These 'Newbies' are unfamiliar with the culture and don't need to know about transport and protocols. In order to bring these new users into the Internet culture quickly, this Guide offers a minimum set of behaviors which organizations and individuals may take and adapt for their own use."

The motivation for the document is clear: to broaden the audience of users from only "insiders"-who had participated in the initial stages of the birth of the Internet-to all those who were accessing it for the first time without any basic expertise or historical and technical preparation about the world they were entering.

With the exponential growth of the Internet since the 1990s and the access of more and more people to the Net, Netiquette has become increasingly important. The same spirit that had moved the drafters from RFC 1855 to its drafting has multiplied into new guidelines, practices, internal documents of companies and organizations, and "codification of rules of conduct" tools of all kinds.

The RFCs themselves have multiplied, going on to focus attention on more and more specific and innovative topics: as of November 2023, the last registered RFC is number 9525, which replaces due to obsolescence RFC 6125 issued in March 2011... regardless of the contents (in this specific case extremely technical and related to standards on protocols for insiders), these numbers give a clear idea of how far we have come since RFC 1855 of 1995 onwards.

Standards have been born, used, and become unnecessary and outdated as the years have passed and the Connected World has expanded, technology has grown, and challenges have multiplied. This is undeniably a field in constant and inexorable transformation.

Online communication has begun to embrace a wide range of platforms, from discussion forums to chat rooms and instant messaging services to the entire universe of social networks, making it necessary to adapt this digital bon-ton to each new innovation.

Companies, too, have come up with their own rules of conduct in the area of digital communications: IT policies, guidelines for the use of social networks, codes of conduct in digital relationships, or even simple rules for how to set up a signature at the bottom of work e-mails.

Exactly like office dress code norms, attention to form in online communications are both methods of showing respect and professionalism in one's everyday context. In some ways, the acceleration toward digital has transformed professional etiquette from "something" that happens within the office walls to "something" that happens on the Internet.

Today it is difficult to hear about "Netiquette." The term is linked to the years of the early Internet boom and is often considered a term peculiar to the generation that saw this phenomenon emerge and develop. As of the date of writing this book, the word "Netiquette" has a very low display rate on major search engines.

This does not mean that Netiquette is dead, but only that awareness of its presence has faded and the perception of it has changed heavily; for "digital natives," some of the notions of computer etiquette its become instinctive, but this should not mislead: it is often the things that are taken for granted that are most needed to be paid more attention to.

The "biases" or cognitive biases represent mental inclinations or predispositions that influence, often in subtle and non-rational ways, our actions, decisions, or instinctive choices. These biases can be regarded as filters through which we interpret reality, and may be rooted in cultural factors, personal experiences, gender stereotypes, age stereotypes, or specificity of the industry in which we operate.

These are thought patterns that, while sometimes useful in rapid decision making, can lead to subjective and unreasonable judgments or attitudes, significantly influencing our behavior and interactions.

In the context of netiquette, biases can have a major impact. For example, assuming that all members of a virtual group share the same cultural background, technological expertise, or communication expectations can lead to misunderstandings, misinterpretations, and, in some cases, unintended exclusions. This can be especially true in diverse work environments where employees of different ages, cultures, or experience levels interact.

A common example of bias in the digital sphere is technology bias related to generational differences, where it is assumed, for example, that younger generations are naturally more proficient in the use of digital technologies, while older generations are less proficient.

This type of assumption can lead to communications that do not take into account the actual skills and needs of all members of a team, creating barriers to understanding and effective communication.

Similarly, cultural biases can influence the tone, language and even timing of digital correspondences, potentially leading to misinterpretation or offense.

Being aware of and actively countering our own biases not only fosters a more inclusive environment, but also improves the clarity and efficiency of our communications.

An ever-evolving art

Netiquette, or digital etiquette, is as we have seen an ever-changing concept, adapting to new platforms and communication needs as they emerge.

The rules governing e-mail communication, for example, do not necessarily apply when using mobile messaging applications ("apps") such as WhatsApp or Telegram, to give examples.

Similarly, norms of behavior on social media can differ greatly from those one should follow during an online business meeting.

The first step to successfully navigating the world of digital politeness is to be aware that each communication channel has its own specifics. Whether it is a corporate chat room, a discussion forum or a social network, each platform-as well as its own regulations-has its own unwritten rules that outline what is considered appropriate or not in that context.

An e-mail will have to adhere to a very different form than a chat message, even if the recipient is the same: the tool governs the behavior and use expected of the user.

By e-mail I could write:
"Hi Luca,
I would appreciate your feedback on yesterday afternoon's meeting.
Thank you."

Netiquette

Via chat I would probably write:
"What did you think of the meeting yesterday afternoon?"

Similarly, a text message prepared to be sent to a friend will have a different tone and form than a text message to be sent to one's principal: thus, it is not only the medium that discriminates the form, but also the recipient.

To a friend maybe I will write:
"ke you do tonight???? ;-)"

To my colleague I will send instead:
"Good morning. What time is the meeting?"

Understanding this nuance is crucial to maintaining positive relationships in the digital world. Adaptability, as in many other aspects of life, is a virtue that should not be underestimated in the workplace-it is a key soft skill.

Soft skills" are interpersonal skills that relate to the ability to interact effectively with others. These skills include communication, listening, empathy and the ability to work in a team. They are critical in the world of work because they affect the quality of professional relationships and the ability to navigate complex environments. While technical skills can be learned through study and practice, soft skills are often developed through personal experiences and interactions.

In addition, "soft skills," tend to be potentially applicable to multiple contexts, unlike "hard skills," that is, specialized, technical skills aimed at specific applications.

To take a simple example, knowing how to drive a truck with a trailer is a hard skill, while knowing how to work calmly in a team is a soft skill. Similarly, knowing computer tools falls under hard skills; taking care to apply the right communication techniques to long-distance relationships is for all intents and purposes a soft skill.

It is not just an isolated skill, but a transferable skill that can have a significant impact on both aspects of our lives: professional and personal.

A great many of our interactions take place online. In a work context, a solid understanding of Netiquette can make the difference between building strong working relationships and incurring unnecessary conflict.Knowing how to formulate a work e-mail respectfully or how to participate in online discussions constructively can be crucial to our professional reputation.

But it is not only in the business world that Netiquette is important, this should be clear In our personal lives as well, a good understanding of the unwritten rules of online communication can improve our interactions and help us build stronger and more rewarding relationships.

Whether it is maintaining an open and respectful dialogue on social media or understanding when it is appropriate to use certain forms of language or emoticons, Netiquette is a skill that goes beyond simple online "know how."

Investing time and effort in understanding the nuances of Netiquette is therefore an investment that pays dividends in both our personal and professional lives. Not only does it make us more adept at navigating the complexities of the digital world, but it also helps build a more respectful and inclusive online environment.

In an increasingly connected world, where the lines between online and offline life are increasingly blurred, being Netiquette savvy is more than just a skill-it is a prerequisite for being a valid Digital Citizen.

Digital Citizenship

Digital Citizenship ("Digital Citizenship " in English), is a concept that embraces the interaction, participation and behavior of people online.

This includes the responsibility and ethics that guide our actions, both as individuals and as members of companies and institutions. In practice, it concerns how we act, communicate and collaborate in the digital world.

It is a topic that is gaining increasing relevance, especially in an age when online life is often becoming almost indistinguishable from offline life.

Similar to how we gain citizenship of a state through active participation, regardless of each nation's specific laws, the digital world also requires active involvement.

We become digital citizens when we actively participate in one or more aspects of this environment. This could include everything from responsible use of social media, to participation in online communities, to ethical use of digital resources.

It is a concept that goes beyond just surfing the Internet; it is a question of how we fit into a larger, interconnected community.

Just as civic sense is fundamental in traditional citizenship, digital citizenship is not just about technology. It also includes how we relate to others online, respect for privacy, information management, and civic engagement in the digital context.

It has become an essential part of our daily lives as technology and connectivity influence more and more aspects of our existence. In this sense, digital citizenship is an extension of our citizenship in the real world, enriched and complicated by the presence of digital tools that can both help and hinder our ability to be responsible citizens.

Digital citizenship promotes open communication and active participation through various channels such as blogs, social media and forums. This kind of participation is the basis for a democratic society, where the free exchange of ideas is a key element.

The ability to express one's opinions, share ideas and participate in debates on relevant issues is made more accessible through technology. This openness is critical to maintaining a healthy society and promoting constructive dialogue in both business and private spheres.

Because of this strong value, digital citizenship emphasizes the importance of digital literacy and technology education. Digital literacy refers to the ability to effectively use digital technologies and platforms to communicate, access information, and solve problems.

In technical terms, it includes a variety of skills ranging from basic knowledge of how to use computers, smartphones, and the Internet, to more advanced skills such as the ability to navigate and evaluate information online, use of office software, understanding of computer security principles, and digital communication skills.

Digital literacy is not only limited to knowing "how" to use technology, but also includes an understanding of "when" and "why" to use it ethically and responsibly. In this sense, digital literacy is critical to participating fully and effectively in today's digital society.

In an age when access to online information and resources is critical, it is also vital that people know how to navigate the digital world safely and consciously.

This includes the ability to assess sources, recognize security threats, and use digital tools effectively. It also involves using strong passwords, being aware of privacy settings and understanding the consequences of sharing personal data.

It is a skill set that should now be developed from a young age, through educational programs that prepare the younger generation to be informed and responsible digital citizens.

Finally, digital citizenship prompts us-or should prompt us-to consider the social impact of our online actions. For example, the spread of false or unverified information can have negative effects on society as a whole: only a proper "civic compass" can help us understand the true consequences of what we do online.

The phenomenon of "keyboard lions" is particularly relevant in this context. This expression refers to individuals who, protected by the anonymity that the screen provides, feel free to act in ways they would normally avoid in the real world.

This false sense of impunity can lead to harmful behaviors such as cyberbullying, spreading unfounded news (so-called *Fake News*) or inciting hatred. In essence, the mindset-the wrong one-is *"I'm not responsible because no one sees me behind the screen anyway."*

Expanding further on this point, the concept that grounds the actions of "keyboard lions" is a distortion of reality that can have serious consequences.

This mindset can fuel a kind of "ethical disengagement," where the person feels disconnected from the social and moral norms that govern behavior in the physical world. This disengagement can manifest itself in various ways: from spreading theories and information without any basis for analysis, to participating in hate speech, to sending threatening messages.

In each case, individuals convince themselves that their online actions will have no real consequences, ignoring the

Netiquette

fact that the digital world is intrinsically connected to the real world and that actions in one space can have repercussions in the other.

Thus, being responsible digital citizens also means thinking about the social consequences of our actions in the digital world. This aspect of digital citizenship is especially relevant at a time when fake news and misinformation can spread rapidly, potentially affecting real events.

Therefore, it is critical that each of us take our role as digital citizens seriously, carefully evaluating the accuracy and impact of the information we share.

Netiquette

Chapter Summary

It is important to understand the meaning of Netiquette and its evolution in the context of digital citizenship. This concept was born when early Internet users realized that the social and behavioral norms of face-to-face communication needed to be adapted to the virtual world, just as there are unwritten rules for manners at social events. Unlike traditional etiquette, rules of behavior online are less commonly learned, although the basic principle of politeness remains the same.

The rapid growth of online relationships has made it necessary to understand how to apply these social dynamics in a distant, virtual context. The phenomenon of "chain letters," insignificant in the Renaissance, is one example. Such letters became a nuisance with the advent of typing, photocopiers, fax machines and, finally, electronic mail, which made it possible to send hundreds of messages quickly and freely.

The netiquette landscape has steadily evolved along with the Internet, adapting to various platforms from e-mail to social networks. Companies have also developed their own digital communication rules, which include policies for computer use, social media and conduct in digital relationships.

Digital citizenship encompasses how people interact, participate and behave online, focusing on responsibility and ethics. It is about our actions as part of a larger digital community, not just Internet browsing. This concept includes respecting others online, managing privacy, managing information, and civic engagement in the digital context. It has become increasingly important as our online and offline lives merge.

Digital literacy is critical to participating effectively in today's digital society and includes not only the use of technology, but also understanding when and why to use it ethically and responsibly. It is critical to navigate the digital world safely and be aware of evaluating sources, recognizing security threats, and using digital tools effectively.

Being a responsible digital citizen also means reflecting on the social consequences of our online actions. In an age of rapidly spreading disinformation, the impact of shared information is significant. "Keyboard lions," on the strength of online anonymity, exemplify the problem of ethical disengagement in the digital space. It is important to assess the accuracy and impact of shared information, emphasizing our role as conscientious participants in the digital world.

Communicating Remotely

Digital Communication

Despite the increasing reliance on technology and the advent of numerous digital communication tools, face-to-face communication maintains an irreplaceable role in the professional and personal world. This type of interaction offers a wealth of nonverbal nuances, such as facial expressions and body language, that are fundamental to full and authentic communication. Face-to-face communication allows for an immediate and personal connection that is often necessary to build trust, empathy, and mutual understanding in a work setting.

However, in an era characterized by globalization and remote working, it is undeniable that interactions via email, chat, and virtual meetings have become fundamental components of working life. These digital tools allow for flexible and immediate collaboration, crossing geographic boundaries and enabling rapid sharing of ideas. Digital communication has transformed the way teams interact and collaborate, enabling greater efficiency and responsiveness in daily operations.

When we interact in person, we have the opportunity to establish a deeper connection with colleagues. Elements such as facial expressions, body language and tone of voice enrich communication, adding a level of understanding and empathy that is difficult to replicate in a digital context.

The elements of communication are mainly divided into three categories: verbal, nonverbal and paraverbal.

Verbal Elements

Word choice in the verbal communication process goes far beyond the simple use of terms. Each word we select has a significant impact on how our message is perceived and interpreted. This process is by no means random, but requires careful thought and sensitivity to the nuances of language.

When we communicate, we are not just assembling words into sentences; we are constructing meanings. Each term we choose carries with it a whole spectrum of meanings and connotations. These aspects can vary widely depending on the cultural context, the specific context of the conversation, and even the emotional state of the listener. Word choice therefore becomes a balancing act: we must consider not only what we want to say, but also how our words will be received.

Nonverbal Elements

They include a wide range of communicative modes that transcend words. These elements, which often operate on a subtle, unconscious level, include body language-gestures, facial expressions, and postures-that can reveal feelings not expressed verbally, or even contradict what is said in words. Body language is a powerful communication tool that, when interpreted correctly, can provide deep insight into a person's emotional states and intentions.

In addition, eye contact is a crucial aspect of nonverbal communication. A look can express a wide range of emotions, from interest and acceptance to challenge or discomfort. Spatial language, which includes how we manage our personal distance and position in a space, also communicates much about our degree of comfort and openness to others. Closer positions may indicate familiarity and comfort, while distance may suggest formality or reserve.

Aspects such as clothing and physical appearance also play a significant role. Clothing can be used to express personal identity, social status, or even membership in a certain group or culture. Physical appearance, including hairstyle and makeup, contributes to first impressions and can influence how others perceive and interact with us.

Paraverbal Elements

Paraverbal elements focus on the way words are expressed, going beyond mere verbal content. The mode of verbal expression, which includes aspects such as tone of voice, rhythm of speech, pauses, emphasis, volume, and intonation, plays a key role in how a message is perceived and interpreted. Tone of voice, for example, can communicate a variety of emotional states, from excitement to frustration, regardless of the words chosen. A calm, measured tone may convey confidence, while a sharp, quick tone may indicate anxiety or excitement.

The pace of speech, that is, the speed at which we speak, can affect the clarity of the message and the listener's ability to follow it. Rapid speech can communicate urgency or passion, while a slower pace can be perceived as thoughtful or even uncertain. Pauses, when used strategically, can emphasize a point, create suspense or give the listener time to absorb complex information.

Emphasis on certain words or phrases is another powerful paraverbal tool. Through emphasis, we can indicate which parts of the message we consider most important, thus influencing the listener's interpretation. In addition, variations in volume, from whispers to high tones, can convey emotional intensity or emphasize the importance of certain points.

Finally, intonation, that is, the variation in the pitch of the voice, is crucial in imparting meaning to words. Intonation can transform a simple statement into a question, an order, or an exclamation, radically changing the perception of the message.

Digital Communication

It is evident that among the three categories of communication-verbal, paraverbal, and nonverbal-only one can be transmitted effectively through channels such as e-mail or chat, namely verbal communication. The inherent limitations of these means prevent the transmission of paraverbal and nonverbal nuances, which are fundamental elements in face-to-face communication.

In the context of a videoconference meeting, however, it is possible to integrate all three components of communication. Thanks to technology, participants can not only hear each other's words, but also see facial expressions and body language, key elements of nonverbal communication. However, even this mode has limitations. The quality of audio in a video conference can, for example, make paraverbal nuances such as tone and volume of voice less clear. In addition, if the video cameras are not turned on, the communication completely loses its nonverbal component, thus limiting the understanding and effectiveness of the message.

To effectively manage remote relationships, it is therefore critical to recognize that remote interactions lack many fundamental aspects of face-to-face communication. This awareness should guide us in how we approach digital communication, taking care not to assume that virtual interactions are equivalent to in-person interactions. The reality is that, despite technological advances, a meeting around a table cannot be replicated exactly in a virtual environment.

This awareness leads us to more productively and ethically consider working relationships through digital platforms. It is important to adapt our communication approach to fill, as much as possible, the gaps left by the absence of nonverbal and paraverbal communication. This may include using clearer, more detailed language in chats or emails and encouraging the use of video cameras during video conferences to preserve some degree of nonverbal communication.

Elements	In Person	E-mail	Online meeting	Chat
Minutes	Yes	Yes	Yes	Yes
Nonverbal	Yes	No	Only with Video	No
Paraverbals	Yes	Limited	Yes	Limited

"Limited" refers to the subtle Paraverbal component consisting of the formatting of the text in the email and the style used in chat.

The Conflicts

In the work environment, strong relationships are a key asset. Personal interactions offer unique opportunities to build trust with colleagues.

Moments such as spending time together outside the office, attending face-to-face meetings, or sharing a lunch are valuable opportunities to deepen mutual understanding. These informal gatherings foster more open and honest

Communicating Remotely

communication, reducing the risk of misunderstanding or conflict.

Nevertheless, conflicts are almost inevitable. Conflicts manifest themselves as disagreements or clashes between individuals or groups arising from differences in opinions, goals, values, or needs: they can arise from a variety of sources, including misunderstandings, lack of clear communication, or rivalry over limited resources. In a professional setting, conflicts are not an uncommon phenomenon; they can arise in any context where people with different perspectives and backgrounds interact.

Important is to recognize that conflicts, although they may create tension, are also natural expressions of diversity and individuality. Their presence in the work environment reflects the variety of thoughts, experiences and expectations that characterize a dynamic and heterogeneous work environment.

When they arise, face-to-face communication is often the most effective way to resolve them. Direct, personal contact allows people to address issues openly, listen to each other's perspectives, and work together to find shared solutions. This approach allows for faster and more lasting resolution of conflicts, preventing tensions that might otherwise linger.

But how to do it if the in-person meeting is not possible?

When face-to-face meetings are not possible, it becomes essential to rely on smart and strategic use of digital technologies to maintain efficiency and connectivity. In an increasingly globalized and interconnected business environment, e-mail, chat, and online collaboration platforms become crucial tools for overcoming physical and time barriers. The ability to select the most appropriate communication tool can have a significant impact, especially in situations of potential conflict or misunderstanding.

For example, let us imagine a situation in which a professional receives a message highly critical of him or her through an e-mail involving several recipients in copy. Instead of responding publicly through the same e-mail, potentially creating further tension or misunderstanding, he might opt for a more direct and personal approach, contacting the interlocutor via chat. This gesture demonstrates a willingness to clarify and resolve the issue quickly and confidentially, avoiding turning a disagreement into a public dispute in front of other colleagues.

This type of approach highlights the importance of understanding the context and emotional impact of different modes of communication. While an e-mail can be effective for formal communications or for sharing information with a large group, chat offers a more immediate and personal channel, ideal for quick discussions or for dealing with sensitive topics discreetly. In addition, chat allows near real-time two-way communication, which is critical for quickly resolving misunderstandings or discussing urgent matters.

Similarly, online collaboration platforms can be used to hold virtual meetings, share documents, and work together on projects, even when team members are spread across different locations. The use of video conferencing, for example, allows a visual dimension to be added to interactions, helping to bridge the gap created by the lack of face-to-face contact.

Choosing the right tool for the right situation not only improves communication and collaboration, but also demonstrates sensitivity and consideration for others, helping to build strong and respectful working relationships, even at a distance.

Adjusting the right tone

In the business context, clarity and accuracy in communication are critical to avoid misunderstandings that can have significant consequences. These misunderstandings can arise when there are discrepancies between the sender's intention and the recipient's interpretation.

It is important to remember that, in face-to-face communication, many nonverbal signals such as facial expressions, gestures and tone of voice play a crucial role in conveying emotional and intentional nuances that complement the verbal message. These elements, however, are absent in written communication, particularly in digital communication, making misunderstandings more likely to occur.

To mitigate this risk in digital communication, it is essential to adopt practices that promote clarity and understanding. The use of clear and direct language, avoiding jargon and ambiguity, is an essential first step.

Structuring the message into well-defined paragraphs and using bullet points can facilitate reading and logical organization of information. This helps separate different topics or key points, making the text not only more readable but also easier to follow.

Even just on an instinctive level, a message like:
"Hello Luca,
I would like to make Andrea more involved in the next meeting, but I don't intend to put too much of a burden on him; therefore, for the next meeting I will only entrust him with the writing of the minutes, and leave the rest to you.
So please proceed to:
- *you set a meeting by the end of the week*
- *You prepare a presentation to share in the meeting*
- *Notify Andrea that he will have to write up the report*

Thank you."

Is definitely more difficult to misunderstand than:
"Hello Luca,
I want Andrea to be more involved in the next meeting, but I don't intend to give him too much of a burden; therefore, for the next meeting I will entrust him with the minutes and leave the rest as usual. Go ahead and do that.
Thank you."

The tone used in digital communications is another element that should not be underestimated. Because tone can be difficult to interpret in a written text, it is critical to use appropriate language. Avoiding overly formal or informal language is advisable, and the use of emoticons or specific expressions can help indicate the desired tone.

This step is extremely complicated: how to address an interlocutor for the first time can indeed be a complex challenge, especially in a professional environment where first impressions are critical. Figuring out the appropriate tone and level of formality in an initial communication requires sensitivity and careful observation.

Tackling the task of setting the right tone in an initial communication with a new interlocutor can be a complex and delicate process. However, by integrating a structured approach system such as from the OODA methodology[2] (Observation, Orientation, Decision, Action), this process can become more structured and manageable.

We start with a "neutral" approach: formal but simple communication. This corresponds to the "Observation" phase of the OODA cycle, where we gather preliminary information about the interlocutor, perhaps through their professional profile, company position, or the context in which the communication is taking place. Here, the goal is to gain an initial understanding of who the interlocutor is and in what kind of context they are communicating.

Next, we move on to the "Orientation" phase. This stage requires interpreting the information gathered during the

---

[2] OODA analysis was developed by USAF Air Force Colonel John Boyd (1927-1997) in the 1950s to help military pilots make quick decisions in high-speed combat situations. In subsequent years, OODA methodology has been applied to a wide range of fields, from industry to technology to politics.

observation. Based on this, the tone to be used in the first message is decided. Neutrality and formality can be safe starting points, avoiding excesses of informality or rigidity that may not be suitable.

Once the first message is sent, we enter the "Decision" phase, where we analyze the response received. Here, the focus is on interpreting the interlocutor's tone, style, and level of formality. This analysis allows us to decide how to adjust our communication style in response.

Finally, in the "Action" stage, we apply the decision made. If the interlocutor's response is formal, we maintain a similar tone. If, on the other hand, it is more informal or relaxed, we can adjust our communication accordingly, while maintaining a level of professionalism appropriate to the context.

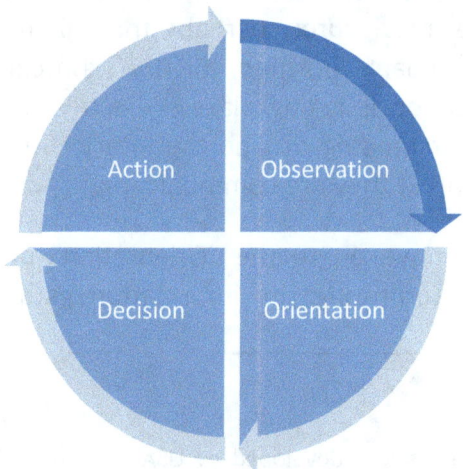

By applying the OODA methodology to communication, we can not only make more informed and strategic choices about how to approach a new interlocutor, but also

Communicating Remotely

dynamically adapt to their responses and the changing context. This approach allows for greater flexibility and more effective communication, helping to establish strong and respectful working relationships from the outset.

To give a practical example, my first email might be:
"Hello Luca,
I am writing to you to get information about file X159, which is stopped at your step. Can you give me an update?
Thank you."

Let us take the case of receiving such a response:
"Hi Debora,
the X159 file has been at a standstill for ages, I don't know what to do anymore, either I'll reject it or I'll never close it!"

At that point my retort would adjust, but still remaining in my own style without copying that of my interlocutor:
"Hi Luca,
thanks for the info. At this point I too would prefer you to reject it so I can create a new one.
Thank you!"

If instead the answer had been:
"Hello Debora,
the file you mentioned has been blocked against me for a long time and there is no action that can resolve it. I can only proceed to formally reject it so as to remove it from my list of activities.
Sincerely."

...I would have adjusted with something like:
"Hello Luca,

I thank you for the clarification. Go ahead and reject file X159 so that I can create a new one.
Have a nice day."

In both cases, my response does not overlap with the tones used by my initial addressee in his or her reply but adapts to them by adjusting my style without distorting it, adapting it to the register chosen by my counterpart. The key must be in the fact that neither I nor the addressee unilaterally fixes the form of the message but adapts it-or should adapt it-to each other's style.

It is also crucial to avoid writing when you are emotionally involved, such as when you are angry or frustrated. Emotions can easily affect the tone of the message and lead to unprofessional communications.

Taking a moment to calm down before responding is always a good practice. The old adage of "*count to ten before responding*" is particularly relevant in this context.

In digital communications, clarity, timeliness, and tone are critical to ensure that the message is interpreted as intended. In a meeting setting, having a clear agenda, a knowledgeable moderator, and a confidential environment are essential elements for effective and productive discussion.

Open dialogue is often the most effective strategy for resolving conflicts. In a digital environment, this might mean a series of confidential, focused message exchanges to understand the positions and concerns of all parties involved. Asking questions to deepen mutual understanding is a key step in this process.

Communicating Remotely

During meetings, negotiation techniques can be used to arrive at solutions acceptable to all. This can include setting clear goals and finding compromises. An experienced moderator can facilitate this process by structuring the discussion to reach agreement.

In spite of all the arrangements made, misunderstandings will always occur, due to the imperfection of the means used to communicate. It is important to be aware of this possibility at all times.

If there is any doubt about the clarity of one's message, or if as a result of a communication received we glimpse the possibility that there may have been a misunderstanding in the exchange, it is always recommended that we delve deeper and clarify the issue.

A quick chat on messaging programs, a phone call on the fly, a quick e-mail taking all other callers out of the copy, for example, can help to better understand whether messages are being correctly understood.

Ethics and Professionalism

Parallel to Netiquette, there is professional ethics: a set of moral and behavioral norms that guide an individual's actions in the work environment. These principles help define what is right or wrong in a professional environment.

Ethics is basically a set of moral principles that guide how people decide and act. It is a branch of philosophy that explores what is considered morally right or wrong, just or unjust, thus influencing human behavior in various circumstances.

This area includes several theoretical approaches. One example is deontology, which emphasizes duties and rules. In the professional world, these deontological principles are manifested through "codes of ethics," which set standards of conduct for those who belong to a professional body.

The interconnection between professional ethics and Netiquette becomes particularly evident in interactions with colleagues and other interlocutors, i.e., "stakeholders," who could, for example, be suppliers or customers, or business functions completely different from our own.

In digital communication, as in e-mail and chat, maintaining ethical behavior is essential. This translates into using polite and professional language and avoiding tones that could be interpreted as accusatory or offensive. For example, it is advisable to avoid excessive use of capital letters, which can be interpreted as virtual shouting. Also, it is important to pay attention to the use of emoticons and abbreviations, making sure that they are appropriate to the professional context and that they are understandable to the recipients.

Virtual meetings, which have become increasingly common, present additional challenges. It is critical to listen carefully and not interrupt other participants. This is not only a sign of good professional ethics, but also a fundamental rule of Netiquette.

In summary, professional ethics and Netiquette are two sides of the same coin, especially in an increasingly digitized world.

Professional ethics provides a general framework on how to behave in a work environment, while Netiquette offers more specific tools for navigating the complicated world of digital interactions.

Finding a balance between these two aspects is critical to building and maintaining a culture of respect, integrity, and professionalism in the modern workplace.

This balance is especially crucial today, when the lines between professional and personal space are increasingly blurred. Online interactions are becoming increasingly significant in our daily work lives. Therefore, it is essential that every professional be equipped not only with a solid understanding of professional ethics, but also with a mastery of Netiquette rules.

This combination of skills is indispensable for successfully navigating the contemporary work landscape, which is characterized by an increasing interconnection between physical and virtual spaces.

In practice, ethics manifests itself in acting with integrity, honesty and respect, profoundly influencing both personal and professional decisions: it constitutes the internal compass that guides us in our choices, whether in small daily actions or in major life issues.

Integrity

Integrity refers to the quality of being honest and having strong moral principles. It manifests itself in consistency between words and actions, acting in accordance with one's values even when no one is watching, and responsibility for one's actions. A person of integrity acts based on what is right and ethical, rather than on what is personally convenient or advantageous.

Integrity begins with honesty, which implies not only truthfulness in words, but also authenticity in actions. It means being true to reality, avoiding deception, lies or manipulation. Moral principles, on the other hand, refer to a set of values and beliefs that guide an individual's decisions and actions. These principles may include justice, fairness, respect for others, and a commitment to do what is morally right.

One of the most distinctive aspects of integrity is the consistency between what a person says and what he does. In other words, a person of integrity not only talks about values and moral principles, but puts them into practice in his or her daily actions. This aligns one's behaviors with one's beliefs, demonstrating consistent fidelity to one's principles.

Integrity is particularly evident when a person chooses to act according to his or her values even when there are no observers. This means making the right choice even when no rewards or recognition are expected and when there are no external consequences for unethical behavior. This authenticity in acting according to one's values, regardless of the situation, is a sign of true character.

A central aspect of integrity is personal responsibility. This involves recognizing and accepting the consequences of one's actions, both positive and negative. A person of "integrity" does not make excuses or blame others for his or her mistakes, but accepts them and seeks to learn and grow from them.

Finally, integrity involves making choices based on what is right and ethical, rather than what is convenient or personally beneficial. This can sometimes mean making difficult decisions or going against the tide, but a person of integrity remains true to his or her moral principles even under these circumstances.

Honesty

At the heart of honesty is the practice of being truthful, which means expressing the truth as one knows it, without omitting or concealing important facts. Being transparent also involves a willingness to share information openly, without trying to deceive or create false impressions. This aspect extends beyond simply avoiding lies, implying proactive honesty and clear, direct communication.

Honesty is manifested in communication that is not only accurate but also sincere and open. This means expressing one's thoughts and feelings genuinely, avoiding masking or manipulating the truth for personal gain. Honest communication builds trust and forms the basis for strong and lasting relationships, both personal and professional.

A fundamental aspect of honesty is acknowledging and accepting one's mistakes. This involves having the courage to admit when one is wrong and taking responsibility for one's actions. This behavior not only demonstrates maturity and integrity, but is also essential for personal growth and maintaining trust in relationships.

Honesty requires presenting facts and information without distortion or exaggeration. This includes avoiding taking information out of context or using it in a misleading way. Presenting facts fairly and impartially is crucial in many areas, from daily life to professional decisions and matters of justice.

Finally, honesty also involves being true to oneself, maintaining authenticity in all interactions. This means living and acting consistently with one's values and beliefs, resisting the temptation to conform to what is false or deceptive in order to please others or for personal gain.

Respect

Respect is a vital component of human relationships and social coexistence. It is a broad concept that implies a range of behaviors and attitudes that recognize and value human dignity. Analyzing and expanding the concept:

Respect begins with treating all individuals with dignity, recognizing that each person deserves consideration and courtesy. This means interacting with others in a way that reflects their inherent humanity and worth, regardless of their personal circumstances, social role or background.

Respect is manifested in recognizing and valuing the diversity and uniqueness of each individual. This is not limited to just tolerating differences, but involves an active appreciation of the various perspectives, experiences and identities that people bring to each context. Recognizing the value of each person contributes to creating an environment in which everyone feels seen and heard.

A key element of respect is listening carefully and considering the opinions of others. This means making space for the voices of others, seeking to understand their views, even when they differ from one's own. Active listening involves genuine attention and a commitment to understanding, rather than simply waiting one's turn to speak.

The principle of treating others as one would wish to be treated is a universal maxim found in many cultures and philosophies. This empathic approach promotes fair and compassionate treatment by encouraging people to put themselves in the shoes of others and consider the effects of their actions on others.

Respect also includes valuing cultural, social and personal differences. In a globalized and multiculturally rich world, understanding and appreciating these differences is critical to building inclusive and tolerant societies. This includes respecting various traditions, beliefs, lifestyles and viewpoints, and avoiding stereotypes or prejudice.

Respect contributes significantly to the creation of environments in which tolerance and inclusion are core values. In such environments, people feel safe in sharing their ideas and identities, knowing that they will be treated with respect and fairness. This fosters collaboration, innovation and a sense of belonging and community.

Chapter Summary

Despite our increasing dependence on technology, face-to-face communication remains irreplaceable for its depth and richness. However, e-mail, chat, and virtual meetings have become indispensable for collaboration, idea sharing, and overall group effectiveness. Efficiently managing remote working relationships is as critical as perfecting direct interactions with colleagues.

Communication is composed of verbal, nonverbal, and paraverbal elements; in long-distance communication, such as e-mail or chat, only the verbal elements can be transmitted effectively. Video conferencing can include all elements, but technological limitations can reduce its impact.

Strong relationships are a key asset in the workplace, and personal interactions offer unique opportunities to build trust. Informal moments such as socializing outside of work, face-to-face meetings, and shared meals foster open communication and reduce misunderstandings or conflict.

Conflicts in the workplace, arising from differences in opinions, goals, values or needs, are almost inevitable. Face-to-face communication is often the most effective method of conflict resolution, as it allows for direct and open discussion. In remote settings, thoughtful use of e-mail, chat, and online collaboration tools can improve efficiency and connectivity. Choosing the right tool is critical to conflict resolution, and an inclusive approach that seeks clarity rather than public confrontation is recommended.

Misunderstandings in the workplace can have significant consequences, often resulting from discrepancies between the sender's intentions and the recipient's interpretations. In digital communication, clarity is achieved with direct language, well-structured messages, and clear paragraphs. Timeliness in communication balances quick responses with the need for thoughtful and accurate responses. Quick responses should not compromise the quality of communication, as hastily crafted messages can create new ambiguities or leave unanswered questions.

The tone of digital communications can be difficult to interpret. It is advisable to use appropriate language and avoid overly formal or informal tones. The tone should fit the style of the recipient while maintaining authenticity. Avoid writing in emotional tones and maintain restraint to ensure professionalism.

Professional ethics, which includes the moral norms that guide actions in the workplace, closely intersects with netiquette in digital interactions. Maintaining ethical behavior in digital communication involves the use of courteous and professional language, avoiding tones that could be perceived as accusatory or offensive. Virtual meetings require careful listening and not interrupting others, which reflects both good professional ethics and netiquette.

Outgoing E-mails

Writing in the Connected World

Email communication is a focal element in our professional lives, a true digital business card that reflects our professionalism and attention to detail. Every e-mail we send fits into a larger context, helping to shape the image others have of us.

This "professional" image is built not only by the words we choose, but also by the way we handle our electronic communication. The clarity of the message, its relevance, and the ability to reach the recipient appropriately are the pillars that support the effectiveness of our e-mail communication.

Like the letterhead used to give the sign of our corporate identity on written communication, an e-mail must mandatorily give this same sense of care for form by using fewer tools and adapting others to the different channel used.

The perception others have of us through our e-mails is something that cannot be underestimated. Effective written communication is a reflection of our competence and professionalism. If neglected, it can lead to a misjudgment of our abilities and work effort.

It is essential to understand that every e-mail sent has the potential to influence our reputation. Therefore, it is essential to focus not only on the content of our communications, but also on how they are perceived by those who receive them.

Writing effective e-mails is a cross-cutting skill that goes beyond simply communicating information. It is an art that requires sensitivity, adaptability, and continual evolution of one's communication skills.

This competence is manifested in the ability to
- Conveying complex messages in a simple way
- Anticipate and respond to the needs of the recipient
- Use the appropriate tone and style for each situation

Being able to communicate clearly and effectively through e-mail not only helps us to be better understood, but also ensures that the value of our work is recognized and appreciated.

Thus, e-mail communication is not a scattered island in the ocean of our work life; rather, it is a bridge that connects the different parts of our professional activity. Clear, well-managed communication can make the difference between a project that proceeds smoothly and one that gets stranded due to misunderstandings. Moreover, the ability to write effective e-mails is a distinctive element that can improve the quality of our work interactions and strengthen professional relationships.

There is nothing worse than doing great work and then seeing it disallowed because of poor communication...or worse yet, to completely ruin it because of a late or incomplete response!

In an increasingly interconnected world where remote work and virtual interactions have become the norm, the ability to communicate effectively via e-mail has become even more significant. In this context, ineffective communication can not only damage the perception of our work, but can also create significant obstacles to our professional growth. A well-written e-mail can be a powerful networking tool, capable of opening doors and creating career opportunities.

After all, our ability to communicate via e-mail is-or should be-directly proportional to our professional success. It is not just a matter of following protocol or adhering to etiquette; it is a fundamental skill that can make the difference between achieving our professional goals or failing to do so.

Considering the importance of this skill, it becomes crucial to devote time and effort to develop and perfect it. It is not just a matter of writing clear and concise messages; it is also a matter of being able to interpret tone, maintain professionalism, and personalize communication to suit the recipient. A well-written e-mail can convey competence, attention to detail and respect for the recipient, which are crucial elements in any professional context.

Investing in the development of this skill not only improves work efficiency, but also enriches the quality of daily interactions. Effective e-mail communication allows you to manage tasks more smoothly, clarify expectations, and build a network of professional contacts based on a solid foundation of trust and mutual understanding. Ultimately, mastery of e-mail communication is an invaluable asset that can positively influence the entire trajectory of a professional career.

The basic elements that define an e-mail are simple but absolutely crucial to its effectiveness and professionalism. These elements are:

Recipients: Each e-mail must have one or more recipients specified. These can be direct (in the "To" field) or indirect (in the "Cc" fields for knowledge copy and "Ccn" for hidden knowledge copy). Clear indication of recipients ensures that the message reaches the correct and intended people.

Subject: The subject line of an e-mail is a brief description or summary of the message content. Although it is technically possible to send an e-mail without a subject line, this is not recommended because it can negatively affect the perception of the message. A missing subject line can make the e-mail look like spam or junk mail, reducing its effectiveness and likelihood of being read. In addition, a well-

Outgoing E-mails

worded subject line contributes to the professionalism of the communication by giving the recipient an immediate idea of the message content and its importance.

Message: The body of the e-mail is where the actual message is transmitted. It can vary in length and format depending on the purpose and recipient of the e-mail. A clear, well-structured and professionally written message is critical to effectively communicate the desired information.

In the absence of any of these three essential elements, an e-mail loses efficiency and professionalism. An e-mail without recipients cannot be sent, one without a subject line risks being ignored or misinterpreted, and one without a message is devoid of content.

The Ideal Recipient

The "recipient" is a key element in any form of communication, be it a letter, message or e-mail. It is the person who receives and interprets the transmitted information. However, the recipient's process of understanding the message is not just a matter of how the information is formulated and sent. The recipient's personal context, which includes his or her past experiences, cultural background, and specific expectations, plays an equally important role.

This dynamic underscores the critical importance of considering the recipient in writing any message. An effective message is one that is written with the reader in mind, not only with the goal of conveying information, but also doing so in a way that is clear, understandable, and relevant to the recipient. This requires an understanding of the recipient's perspective, their potential needs, and the best way to reach them.

Having clarity about who will receive our message allows us to tailor the tone, style, and even structure of the content so that it is most effective. This is critical in any form of communication, but it becomes even more crucial in contexts such as e-mail and chat, where nonverbal nuances of communication are absent and each word can have a significant impact on the perception and interpretation of the message.

In "To"

The e-mail recipient is a required piece of information for sending the message, without which no e-mail will ever be sent from your e-mail program or system.

Its importance, however, is not reduced to a mere formal obligation: to send the message it is enough to accurately identify which -or which- contact information should be included as primary recipients (in "To") but for the e-mail to be truly effective it is even more important to identify it correctly.

All persons who take an active part in the discussion, that is, those who without that e-mail cannot perform an activity or who as a result of that e-mail must take an action in relation to its content, are considered recipients of the communication.

The message is directed to them and the information contained is essential for them, or it is essential for us that one or more of them give answers to the questions in the text (or give opinions, permissions, and the like).

To summarize: the e-mail should be sent "in To" (i.e., with recipient in the "To" field or whatever label for the primary recipient) to everyone who needs to "do something" with the information in the message.

In "CC"

The field "cc" or "carbon copy" ("carbon copy" in English) or similar names is reserved for second-level recipients, those for whom no action is required in the message, but who might be interested in learning about the subject matter.

The simplest case is, for example, to make one's boss aware, so that he knows what is going on and, in case in the future the issue creates problems, he is able to have a "history" of the situation among his e-mails.

This area of the message is the one that contains the greatest pitfalls: while figuring out who needs to act and needs to be put "in To" is easy, drawing up the list of people who might be interested can be complicated and lead to mileage results.

Absurdly, then, the analysis of "copy recipients" requires a specific and thorough analysis: if I enter in cc my superior, for example, should I also enter that of the colleague to whom I am writing (the colleague "in To")?

I, personally, follow what I call "the rule of three."

- to the third unanswered email, I copy the superior of the recipient(s).
- to the third email without having resolved the problem or seeing any progress in its resolution, I add in cc my superior
- on the third aggravation of the situation (obviously if it has not become a critical issue, but only if there is an exacerbation of the problem), I put my supervisor and the recipient's supervisor

This only helps me to understand whether to include the next hierarchical rank in the communication circle, but certainly not to identify all the functions involved.

This simple question opens a whole chain of reflections on hierarchy, etiquette, and relationships between functions.

In order to figure out which departments or business stakeholders other than my own to put in copy, there is no precise matrix, other than an assessment of multiple factors that balance the severity and urgency of the issue being handled and the addition of stakeholders: the more urgent an issue is, the more downstream functions will need to be included in the process to optimize the time it takes for communications to pass.

The use of the "cc" (carbon copy) function in e-mails proves particularly useful in various work situations, such as during periods of absence or scheduled replacements. When an employee knows that he or she will be absent for a period of time, such as during vacation, carbon-copying the colleague who will assume his or her responsibilities can ease the transition. In this way, the colleague who takes over will have

Outgoing E-mails

access to all relevant e-mails and will therefore be better prepared to handle tasks during the absence.

Similarly, when an employee fills in for a colleague, keeping the latter in carbon copy in sent messages can be advantageous. This practice allows the absent colleague to have a complete record of the communications made on his behalf. When he or she returns, he or she can then resume work with a clear view of the activities performed during his or her absence.

In "BCC"

The "blind carbon copy" is the field that allows a recipient to be added invisible to all other receivers in "To" or in "CC"

Not always enabled by default in mail clients, it is however easy to enable it with a few clicks in most email software, usually through the "option" functions of the message itself.

Hidden copying allows you to add one or more recipients secretly: for example, let your colleague know without all recipients knowing, so that he can read the e-mail but not receive any responses that will come from the initial recipients.

The disadvantage of the BCC field lies in the fact that the person who will receive the email in a hidden copy will have to be well aware of this function and how it works: think of the case when the hidden recipient presses the "Reply to All" button without realizing that the others do not know about his presence in the communication!

The BCC field is a section to be used sparingly: personally, I use it exclusively in case I need to add my superior "in the know" to an e-mail that is not meant to be or seem aggressive or official.

For example, if I have to let a client know that he will be receiving an official communication from my boss shortly, I put the boss himself in BCC so that it is clear that the e-mail I sent has no official status and that I am certainly not soliciting my boss...but BCC allows me to let him know that I have sent a notice.

An often used and extremely useful function of BCC, however, is sending the same e-mail to different recipients without them being able or required to read the other addresses involved.

For example, if I were to send a service notice to all my suppliers, I would have only two options: send an e-mail to each of them or send a single e-mail with all their contact information in hidden copy so as not to "spread" it among them by giving each one visibility of the other's e-mail address.

Although widely used, I have personally encountered many problems with this practice for "commercial" purposes: who receives the email, if he or she does not read his or her address among the "in To" recipients of the email, may consider the message a SPAM without even reading it carefully, or may feel diminished anyway by not having received a targeted email. Nevertheless, it remains an extremely useful tool for quick and confidential mailings.

Outgoing E-mails

One of the major concerns related to the use of BCC is usually privacy. While it allows e-mail addresses to be kept hidden, however, this feature can also raise issues regarding transparency in communications.

It is critical to be aware of how and when to use BCC to avoid misunderstandings or trust issues.

The Art of the Object

Needless to say, the Subject field is a vital part of every e-mail and therefore must not only be present, but must also be used strategically. The brevity of the content of the Subject field in an e-mail message is of crucial importance.

Keeping the subject concise makes the message more effective. This rule is supported mainly by two factors:
- A verbose object tends to be less read in its entirety. Second, an overlong object may present problems when it comes to saving it locally or to cloud storage services that have restrictions on the number of characters in the file name.
- It is essential to be aware of the character limits imposed by archiving services, both local and cloud. This is because, when an e-mail message is saved for archiving purposes, a file is created whose name corresponds to the Subject of the message. Ignoring this detail could lead to inconvenience in the archiving process by our receivers.

The first point deserves special attention. The attention threshold of interlocutors varies from person to person, but it tends to decrease steadily for everyone. This dynamic should influence the writing of any text, starting with the subject of the message.

A well-formulated subject line can make all the difference in capturing the recipient's attention and ensuring that the message is read and considered. In an age when people are inundated with a constant stream of information, effectively capturing the recipient's attention is more important than ever. Whether it is a social media post or the subject line of an email, the initial element must be interesting and catchy enough to interrupt the recipient's normal flow of attention and grab his or her interest.

The Hook

A digression into the social media universe can perhaps help clarify the concept by analyzing the logic of the so-called "hook[3]". A "hook" in social media is a catchy initial element in a post or video that immediately captures the user's attention and encourages him or her to continue reading or

---

[3] The concept of "hook" as we know it today in marketing and media cannot be attributed to a single inventor, since it is an evolution of advertising and psychological techniques that have developed over many years. However, the term "hook" in the context of writing and marketing is often discussed in relation to Nir Eyal (Israel 1980), author of the book "Hooked: How to Build Habit-Forming Products," published in 2014.

Outgoing E-mails

viewing. It can be an intriguing sentence, a striking image, a curious fact or a provocative question.

The primary goal of a hook is to stimulate interest and curiosity by inviting users to interact more deeply with the content. This can mean reading an entire post, watching a video to the end, or actively participating through likes, comments, or shares. An effective hook creates an immediate impact, making the content more memorable and engaging.

In the highly competitive social media environment, where users are constantly bombarded with a wide range of content, an effective hook is critical to stand out and engage the audience.

Similarly, in the world of professional communications, as in the case of e-mail, the subject line takes on a role similar to that of a hook in social media. In an environment where professionals receive dozens or hundreds of e-mails a day, a well-formulated subject line can make the difference between a message that is opened and read and one that is ignored. A good email subject line should be clear, concise and directly related to the content of the message, giving the recipient a reason to engage with the email received.

A good practice is to begin the subject with the most relevant information. These can be presented in aggregate form, separated by a hyphen or other easily recognizable symbol. This approach helps to immediately capture the recipient's interest.

For example, instead of using an object such as

Outgoing E-mails

"Quite urgent question on order 54321 regarding the quantity that can be supplied soon and the minimum delivery time"

it would be more effective to opt for something like
"Urgent - Ord.54321 - Time and Quantity"

In summary, the wording of the subject line in an e-mail message is something that should not be overlooked. Brevity and clarity are essential to ensure not only that the message is read, but also that it can be filed effectively.

Also not to be underestimated is the impact of a concise and effective subject line on the reader's memory: considering that an email can be searched and found even after months and still make itself immediately identifiable is crucial when choosing a practical and distinctive subject line.

Keeping in mind the attention threshold of stakeholders and the technical limitations of archiving services, the effectiveness of e-mail communication can be optimized.

With careful planning and consideration, the subject line of an e-mail can serve as a powerful tool for improving the quality and effectiveness of professional communication.

The Actual Message

The Email Message, or "body of text," consists of a few basic parts that, in strict order, shape the communication we are sending:

1. Initial greetings
2. The introduction

3. The Text
4. The possible request for action
5. Final greetings
6. The Signature

Each of these sections must always be present (excluding the call to action if the e-mail is informational only) in order for the message to be considered complete.

Initial greetings

An e-mail should start with a greeting. Whether it is a simple "Good morning" or not, it is good manners to always start with a greeting.

In the days when we were still talking about typing and not word processing, it was taught that business letters began with "Dear Mr./Mrs." followed by the name, a comma and a "carriage return."

I still follow this "visual" construction, but I have long since replaced the very formal and impersonal "Gentile" with other types of greetings and removed the gender designation altogether:

"Hello Luca,   *"Good   morning   "Good   morning*
I write to..."   *Luca,*   *Luca,*
                      I write to..."   *I write to..."*

How to address the interlocutor

Outgoing E-mails

The formality of language must be appropriate to the context and the recipient. While an overly informal tone may seem unprofessional, overly formal language can create unnecessary distance.

It is crucial to strike the right balance, adapting the tone according to the relationship with the recipient and the nature of the message, as we have already seen in previous chapters.

It is usually a good idea to indicate a title only if we are fully aware that it is the correct one and reporting it in its shortened form: no "Doctor" to anyone regardless, but a respectful "Eng." when we are certain that the person we are writing to is actually an engineer, for example.

Among colleagues belonging to the same organization, the use of the name during a conversation can have several positive effects. Among these, the most obvious is the creation of a climate of mutual respect and recognition as members of the same team, amplifying the sense of belonging.

This approach can also be applied to regular suppliers and customers to whom we want to convey a sense of "partnership," of collaboration.

For the first email to be sent to an associate or business partner, this is my preferred form. Once a relationship is established, it is the exchange of messages that will help us understand how to properly address each recipient.

This detail is also important to remember: once message exchanges become frequent and acquaintance deepens, it will be almost natural to change the forms of greetings, adapting them to a proper balance between our style and that of the specific receiver.

Obviously for foreign language emails, especially in English, the possibility of the use of "she" falls away, but not the issue of respect due through form and substance. It is essential to always keep clear the type of register we decide to use based on the "closeness" with the recipient.

The introduction

The effectiveness of an e-mail begins with its opening. The first paragraph of the text-or, better yet, the first line-should encapsulate all the basic data about the sender and the context in which the message is set.

Although the official details, contacts and titles of the writer are often present in signatures, it is quite intuitive that a signature is the last thing that will be read: should I force the recipient to find out only at the last minute who he or she is talking to?

Exactly as in a face-to-face meeting, introduction is the first step: detailing who is writing and why they are doing so is a necessary act of courtesy both for e-mails sent to new recipients and for messages that might be forwarded to unknown recipients who will therefore find it convenient to find out the history of the message from the beginning.

"Hello,

I am in charge of tracking expiring orders on customer job order code15872.
Can you check the list of the most urgent purchase orders that you still have on file?"

A few words at the beginning of the message to clearly and immediately detail the writer's role or activity can make an e-mail exponentially clearer and therefore more effective, while also empowering the reader to use it within his or her own organization without having to add introductions or preambles to our request.

This last point is crucial: even if the e-mail is intended for one of our regular contacts, it is always education to add context at the beginning of the text so that anyone reading can understand the scope of the communication.

For example, a message like.
"Luca, will you turn the rush orders over to me?"

in the eyes of an external reader is much less transparent than
"Luca, I'm writing to you about the orders that are due: can you turn me the list of the most urgent orders?"

In this way, if our regular recipient is absent or forwards the message to his or her colleagues, the setting of the message ("orders due") will remain very clear even though usually our interlocutor would know it very well.

The Text

An e-mail is not a mystery novel in which to reveal the plot bit by bit: a professional communication or document must be about optimizing the reader's time and maximum transparency.

Writing an effective e-mail requires incorporating the six basic questions of Anglo-Saxon journalism and fiction: Who, What, When, Where, Why and How[4] . These elements provide a clear and comprehensive structure, ensuring that the message is not only informative, but also easily understood by the recipient.

1. **Who:** This element addresses both the recipient(s) of the communication and the key actors mentioned in the message. Clearly identifying who is involved or who needs to be informed is essential to ensure that the message reaches the right people and that responsibilities are clear.

2. **What:** This is the subject of the message. Whether it is an update, a request, or an invitation, it is important to clearly define the purpose of the message. This helps the recipient immediately understand the focus of the communication and the importance of it.

---

[4] It is the 5W+1H rule, or the Kipling Method from a line in the book "The Curious Little Elephant" published in 1902 by British author Rudyard Kipling (Bombay 1865-London 1936), in which he expresses, "I have six honest servants who have taught me everything I know; their names are What and Why and When and How and Where and Who."

Outgoing E-mails

3. **When:** If the e-mail is tied to a specific deadline, event, or timeline, it is critical to specify these details. Providing a clear time context helps avoid confusion and ensures that all parties are aligned on timing. Adding chronological placement can also be important to help various stakeholders better understand the overall context.

4. **Where:** This element specifies the geographic location or context related to the message. Providing precise location details helps recipients better organize their participation or interaction and ensures that all parties are coordinated regarding the physical or digital location needed.

5. **Why:** The reason for the communication. This explains the context and relevance of the message, providing the recipient with a deeper understanding of the motivation behind the communication. This aspect can be critical in motivating the action or response and giving clarity to the message.

6. **How:** Includes details on how the recipient should respond, who to contact for further information, or the next steps planned. This aspect provides clear guidelines and can be critical to the effectiveness of the action that follows the communication.

Integrating these five elements into an e-mail not only improves the clarity and effectiveness of the message, but also demonstrates professionalism and attention to detail. This structured approach ensures that all important information is presented in a logical and easily accessible manner, increasing the likelihood that the message will be received correctly and appropriately.

To give an example:
"Hello everyone,
I am writing from the finance office: we are expecting by Friday from the Purchasing Department an e-mail with the list of open orders in Excel format so that we can check any pending orders.
Thank you."

- *Who: the Purchasing Department*
- *What: Making the order list*
- *When: By Friday*
- *Where: Via e-mail*
- *Why: To control slopes*
- *How: In Excel format*

Clarity and Conciseness

Professional e-mail writing is a skill that rests on two fundamentals: clarity and conciseness. In business, clarity is a key determinant of effective communication.

The primary goal in writing an e-mail is to make the message easily understandable to the recipient. Structuring the content into logical, well-organized paragraphs greatly improves both readability and comprehensibility of the text.

So-called "walls of text are messages consisting of blocks of words with no spacing between paragraphs, very long sentences and an obvious visual burden on the reader.

Even at first glance, a Wall of Text instinctively involves a greater effort of concentration to even keep track of the line we are reading, in the sea of dozens of lines that fill the

> Text walls are those long blocks of text that often appear in emails, documents, or online posts where there is a lack of breaks such as paragraphs, bulleted lists, or spacing that could make the text more readable and organized at first glance a wall of text can seem daunting and difficult to follow because the reader has to struggle to distinguish where one idea ends and another begins without the visual aid of paragraph or list breaks this can make understanding the content more challenging especially if the text is dense with complex information or concepts also the lack of structure can make it difficult for the reader to maintain concentration and follow the flow of the discourse in some cases walls of text may be used intentionally to convey a feeling of overload or to reflect a stream of consciousness in which thoughts are expressed continuously and uninterruptedly however in most professional and academic contexts it is recommended to avoid walls of text in favor of clearer formatting.

reading area.

The visual organization of an e-mail is a key aspect that contributes greatly to its readability and comprehension. Using separate paragraphs, switching to a new line at the end of each concept, or using bulleted or numbered lists are essential techniques for making the text more accessible and easy to read.

1. **Spaced** paragraphs: Separating paragraphs creates a visual space between different topics or sections of the message. This helps the recipient easily distinguish and assimilate each part of the content, making reading less strenuous and more organized. Well-defined paragraphs make it easier to scan the text and allow the reader to find relevant information quickly.

2. **Go "wrap up" at the end of concepts:** Inserting a pause or starting a new line at the end of each key

concept helps segment the message into more manageable units of thought. This approach guides the reader through the flow of information, enabling better understanding and making it easier to remember the main points.

3. **Visible lists:** Using bulleted or numbered lists to highlight key points, passages, or elements of a list makes the text immediately more usable. Lists help break down information into smaller, easily digestible parts, making it easier for the reader to focus on each item without being overwhelmed by a continuous block of text.

The choice of language is another critical aspect. The use of overly technical or complex terms should be avoided unless it is certain that the recipient is aware of and has mastered those terms.

Again, however, as with initial introductions, it is always good to remember that the e-mail may be forwarded to third parties whose knowledge may be less than ours and that of our original recipient: avoiding excessive technicalities facilitates this transmission of information.

Simple, direct language often proves to be the most effective strategy for ensuring that the message is easily understood. Even the use of acronyms, however well known or widespread in one's organization they may be, is to be avoided on a par with excessive technicalities.

"Have you read the Minute of Meeting?"
is to be preferred to

"Have you read the MOM?"

If an acronym is really necessary, perhaps because the term is repeated several times in the text, it should always be the sender's care not to assume that all receivers know it, and it is therefore necessary to include an explanation of it in the message itself.

For example:
"Have you read the Minute of Meeting (MOM)?
In this MOM, I implemented speaker tracking for each speech, unlike the MOMs of previous meetings."

Concision is of equal importance to clarity, especially in a work environment where time is a limited resource. Avoiding repetition of information and focusing on essential details is critical.

Anecdotes or details not directly related to the main topic should not be included. Adopting short, direct sentences helps to keep the message concise, minimizing the risk of possible misunderstandings.

A crucial step in the drafting process is rereading the text before sending. This step allows you to assess the effectiveness of each word and phrase used, removing any superfluous elements that could weigh down the message. This expedient helps to maintain the clarity and conciseness of the text.

The Form!

In written communication, especially in a professional or formal context, adherence to correct grammar and syntax is crucial. The appropriate use of capitalization and punctuation is not only a matter of grammatical correctness, but also conveys professionalism and attention to detail.

Whether it is English or a foreign language, it is important to respect the grammar and writing rules specific to that language. This shows respect for the recipient and for the language itself, as well as ensuring that the message is clear and easily understood.

Common mistake in e-mail writing is lack of proofreading. Careful proofreading can help identify and correct typos or grammatical errors that could compromise the clarity of the message or give the impression of carelessness.

Basic Rules to Remember:

- Beginning of Sentences and Proper Names: The beginning of every sentence and proper names should begin with a capital letter. This not only follows grammatical rules, but also makes it easier to read the text.

- Proper Use of Exclamation and Question Marks: Excessive exclamation or question marks, or their improper use, can alter the tone of the e-mail, making it too informal or even aggressive. It is important to balance the use of these signs to maintain a professional tone.

- Importance of Commas: The correct use of commas is crucial to avoid ambiguity and confusion. Commas are used to separate elements in a list or to insert natural pauses, contributing to the clarity and fluidity of the text. The comma is used to separate elements in a list, to isolate incises or explanatory phrases, and to create a break in the reading. It is important not to use the comma between subject and verb, except in specific cases, such as in the presence of an aside.

- Spaces after Punctuation: A space should be left after each punctuation mark, such as periods, commas, semicolons, colons and ellipses, before starting the next word. However, a space should not be left before punctuation marks. For example, you write "This is a sentence." not "This is a sentence ." Also, after the period that closes a sentence, leave a space before starting the next sentence.

    The only exception is parentheses: the "opening" parenthesis of juxtaposes with the word that follows it, to better enclose the sentence it contains. So not "The (French) Society," nor "The (French) Society," but "The (French) Society."

- Length and Complexity of Sentences: Sentences that are too long and complex or have convoluted structures can make the text difficult to read and understand. It is advisable to use concise and clear sentences to improve readability and ensure that the message is understood correctly.

Other useful points:
- Bulleted Lists and Capitalization: When creating bulleted lists, each item should begin with a capital

letter if each item is a complete sentence or an independent statement. If the bullet points in the list are parts of a larger sentence, start with lowercase.

- <u>End of Sentences:</u> Each sentence should end with a period. Sentences without periods can mistakenly blend together, making the text difficult to follow and understand.

- <u>Use of Suspension Dots (Three Dots):</u> Suspension dots, represented by three consecutive dots ("..."), are used to indicate a pause in speech, an interruption, the omission of a part of the text, or a leaving something unsaid or implied. It is important not to use more or less than three dots for this function. Suspension dots do not have to be followed by a comma, semicolon, or period, but they can be followed by a question mark or exclamation point if the sentence calls for it (although this is strongly discouraged in professional settings).

The possible request for action

A "Call To Action" (CTA), or Request for Action, is a strategic element used in various communication contexts, particularly in marketing, business communications, and professional e-mail. Its main purpose is to incentivize the recipient to take a specific action. Here is a detailed analysis of the concept:

A CTA is a phrase or command that clearly invites the recipient to take an immediate and specific action. This action can be of various kinds, such as responding to e-mail, visiting a Web site, downloading a document, signing up for a service, purchasing a product, or attending an event.

To make it effective, the CTA must be highly visible, clear and unambiguous, both to the primary recipient and to other readers in copy.

The visibility of a CTA is improved by strategically placing it in the e-mail. Ideally, it should be toward the end of the body of the message, immediately after the presentation of relevant information, but obviously before the salutation and signature.

This position ensures that the reader, after absorbing the essential content of the e-mail, immediately encounters the call to action, encouraging them to respond promptly.

Clarity is another key aspect. The CTA must concisely and precisely express what is expected by the recipient.

For example, instead of using vague phrases such as "*We await a response*," more direct and specific wording such as "*Please confirm participation by [date]*" is preferable. This not only makes the request clearer, but also sets a deadline, increasing the likelihood of a timely response.

Clarity of the CTA is ensured by avoiding ambiguity in both language and expectations. The CTA must be worded so that there is no doubt about the required actions.

If the CTA requires clicking on a link, for example, it is helpful to provide context about why and what to expect from the link, thereby increasing trust and the likelihood that the recipient will follow through with the request.

It should not be forgotten that if there are many recipients in the email, it is essential to indicate exactly which actor each CTA is intended for. No doubts should arise for those reading the message in understanding "who" will have to do "what" as a result of receiving it:

"@Andrea, please send us the report as soon as it is ready."

"We await the report from Andrea by the end of the week."

"By the end of the week, the report should arrive (by Andrea)"

Final greetings

As with initial greetings, final greetings should be in harmony with the overall tone of the communication. In a formal, professional context, phrases such as "Sincerely Regards" or "Best Regards" convey a sense of respect and formality.

Instead, in less formal situations or with recipients with whom a more confidential relationship has been established, a "Dear Greetings" or simply "Greetings" may be appropriate, offering a more personal and friendly tone.

It is also important to consider the culture and norms of the recipient. For example, in some international contexts, greeting formulas such as "*Best regards*" or "*Kind regards*" may be more appropriate because they are commonly recognized and accepted in a global business context.

Choosing the right greeting reflects not only an understanding of social conventions but also cultural sensitivity.

In addition, consistency between the initial and final greetings is critical. If the email begins with a formal tone, the final salutation should maintain the same formality. This consistency helps build a cohesive and professional message from beginning to end.

Final greetings are also an opportunity to reaffirm one's availability or for a call to action, such as when expecting a response or further interaction.

A phrase such as "*I remain available for any clarification*" or "*Awaiting your kind reply*" not only closes the message, but also signals a next stage of interaction, keeping the line of communication open.

The Signature

The signature in an e-mail serves as a digital business card. The signature in an e-mail is like the business card we leave at the end of a meeting: it should communicate who we are, what position we hold, and how we can be contacted.

Clarity is the fundamental principle of effective signing. The position or role within an organization should be immediately apparent. This aspect not only expresses professionalism, but also provides the recipient with clear context about the nature of the communication.

A signature that clearly specifies the role, such as "*Purchasing Manager*," provides an instant understanding of the position held by the individual.

It is essential to include contact details while keeping it simple. Elements such as phone number, e-mail address, and links to professional profiles are appropriate. An overly loaded signature can distract and detract from professionalism: quotes, excessive graphics, redundant links may be out of place.

The signature should reflect the corporate image. Elements such as corporate logos or distinctive colors, if used discreetly, can reinforce the corporate brand. It is important, however, to avoid graphic excesses or inappropriate fonts that may compromise readability and professionalism.

For an image, such as a company logo, to be visible directly within the body of an e-mail, it is necessary that both the e-mail sending and receiving programs support the HTML format[5]. HTML e-mails allow the inclusion of images, complex layouts, custom text styles, and other graphic elements that are not possible in a plain text format.

---

[5] HTML, an acronym for HyperText Markup Language, is the standard formatting language for creating Web pages and Web applications born in 1990 and still the cornerstone of website and e-mail formatting.

Outgoing E-mails

Although most modern e-mail clients support HTML format, there is no guarantee that all recipients will have this formatting enabled. Some users may prefer or be limited to mail clients that display messages only in plain text format, due to personal preferences, security settings, software limitations, or other reasons.

When an HTML message is received by a mail program that supports only the text format, images will not be displayed directly in the body of the e-mail. These images are often turned into separate attachments. This can make the message less intuitive and more difficult for the recipient to interpret because the images are not integrated into the context of the message.

For this reason, I personally avoid images in my e-mail signatures so that I do not have concerns about how my recipient will receive message and image.

Nevertheless, corporate guidelines might stipulate otherwise: complying with the rules and practices of one's organization should always take priority.

Adding a legal disclaimer or confidentiality notice may also be required by your company and relevant, especially in areas where sharing sensitive information is common. These elements help define the tone and legal context of the communication.

It is important that the signature be adaptable to different contexts. In some situations, a reduced version of the signature may be preferable, especially in long e-mail exchanges or internal communications where extensive details may not be necessary.

In the absence of rules dictated by our organization, the basic guidelines then are:

- first and last name as the first line of the signature
- clear professional role
- contacts divided by type
- no pictures
- no quotes or comments
- no excess colors or fonts

Chapter Summary

Email is a vital component of professional life, as it serves as a digital business card that reflects our professionalism and attention to detail. Each e-mail contributes to others' broader perception of us. Effective written communication is based not only on the words we choose, but also on how we handle our electronic communication, emphasizing clarity, relevance, and appropriateness of the message.

Writing effective e-mail is a skill that goes beyond simply conveying information. It involves sensitivity, adaptability and continually evolving communication skills. Key skills include simplifying complex messages, anticipating and responding to recipients' needs, and using the appropriate tone and style for each situation. Clear and effective communication via e-mail ensures that our work is understood, recognized and appreciated.

Email communication is not isolated in our professional lives, but acts as a bridge connecting different aspects of our professional activities. Clear and well-managed communication can make the difference between a project running smoothly and one hampered by misunderstandings. Effective e-mail communication is a distinctive element that can improve the quality of our work interactions and strengthen professional relationships.

Understanding the recipient is critical to effective communication. The message must be crafted with the reader in mind, taking into account his or her context, past experiences, and expectations. The e-mail should be sent to all active participants in the discussion or to those who need to take action based on the content of the e-mail.

The body of the e-mail should consist of several key elements: opening salutation, introduction, main text, possible call to action, closing salutation, and signature. Each section plays a crucial role in conveying the message effectively and professionally.

Emails should be clear and concise, avoiding long, complex sentences that can generate misunderstandings. Clear and direct language helps ensure that the message is understood, and the e-mail should answer the basic questions: who, what, when, why, and how.

Proper grammar and syntax are essential for professional e-mail communication. This includes the correct use of capitalization, punctuation and sentence structure, which not only follows grammar rules but also conveys professionalism.

The e-mail signature serves as a digital business card, providing essential contact information and reflecting the sender's professional identity. It should be clear, concise and reflect the image of the organization, avoiding unnecessary graphics or excessive information. Depending on the industry and company policies, legal disclaimers or confidentiality notices may be required in the e-mail signature, particularly when sharing sensitive information.

Inbound E-Mails

The Digital Organization

Without efficient management, the inbox can easily degenerate into a cluttered and overloaded environment where it becomes difficult to distinguish important communications from less urgent ones. This digital chaos can result in considerable wasted time and inefficiencies in workflow, with important messages getting lost in the sea of uncategorized e-mail.

To prevent this scenario, adopting a system of labels or tags is an extremely effective strategy. These tags function as a powerful categorization tool, allowing e-mails to be organized in a systematic way. One can, for example, create distinct groups of e-mails based on various criteria, such as the project to which the e-mail relates, the internal department involved, or the degree of urgency and priority of the message.

The implementation of specific categories for different work areas facilitates a more rational organization of the mailbox. This allows important messages to be quickly identified and responded to in a more targeted and efficient manner. For example, separate labels can be created for each ongoing project, for internal and external communications, for urgent requests, or for informational e-mails such as newsletters or company updates. This type of organization helps not only to reduce inbox clutter, but also to improve time management and prioritization.

In addition, most modern e-mail systems offer advanced features that support the use of categories or labels to sort and archive various incoming messages. These features can also include automated rules that assign specific labels to e-mails based on certain criteria, such as the sender, keywords in the subject or message body. Automation further facilitates e-mail management, allowing users to focus on the most relevant messages without having to spend excessive time manually organizing their inbox.

Establishing an efficient priority system is a focal step in effective e-mail management. With the sheer volume of communications that crowd e-mail inboxes on a daily basis, being able to quickly distinguish between messages of varying importance is critical. Many modern e-mail platforms offer the ability to mark e-mails as important or urgent, often through the use of stars, flags or other distinctive symbols. This feature is particularly useful for highlighting those

Inbound Emails

communications that need immediate attention and response, separating them from the flow of less critical information.

The use of these priority indicators can transform inbox management into a more orderly and focused process, where the most important e-mails are recognized and treated with the celerity they require. One can, for example, set up filters or rules that automatically move these messages to a dedicated folder or highlight them so that they stand out visually when the inbox is opened.

However, it is essential to exercise discretion in the use of these priority signals. If every message is marked as urgent or important, it creates a diluting effect on the value of these indicators. In a sea of e-mails labeled "*Urgent,*" the true sense of urgency is lost, making it difficult to identify those communications that truly require immediate action. In addition, overuse of these indicators can lead to a sense of overload and anxiety, with the result that even truly critical messages may not receive the attention they deserve in a timely manner.

For optimal management, it is advisable to use these priority markers in a strategic and considered manner. Setting clear criteria on what constitutes actual "urgency" can help avoid abuse of these tools. For example, you might decide to reserve the "important" marker only for emails that require action within the next 24 hours or for those that come from superiors or key customers.

Very useful are the customizable categories, with which we can literally label each group of messages by homogeneous groups.The best way to take advantage of this tool is to study at the desk the subdivisions and titles under which we have an interest in identifying our communications, create the "labels" on the post client, and then apply them by hand or through automation (such as and Outlook "rules") in a consistent manner.

The search function is also a powerful tool for quickly finding the information you need. Using search filters for keywords, dates, sender, or attachment size can save valuable time that would otherwise be spent scrolling through long chains of messages.

This is one of the reasons why the subject line is a key key: from the perspective of an inbox search, in fact, it is quite obvious that a well-written subject line makes it extremely easy to recognize the e-mail among all the other search results.

Email archiving is one method of keeping the inbox tidy. Instead of leaving all messages in the inbox, you can archive those that do not require immediate action or that involved actions we have already taken. This keeps the inbox focused on current tasks, while less urgent information remains easily accessible for future reference.

As a practical matter, I leave in "inbox" only those e-mails that I have not yet handled or have yet to work on, and I archive in subfolders divided by subject matter everything that I have "closed," that is, done in its entirety (including having already sent a reply to the sender).

Inbound Emails

Emails on which I have yet to take action are also categorized by topic or urgency using Microsoft Outlook categories, so that I can find the outstanding workload for each of the tasks as quickly as possible.

Finally, automation is an advanced vision that can significantly improve e-mail management. Setting up rules that automatically filter and organize incoming messages can save time and reduce stress. These rules can be customized to meet the specific needs of each user, ensuring that the inbox is always organized. Understanding the functions of your mail client is vital to understanding its potential in this regard.

It is important to regularly review and update your e-mail management system. As job responsibilities change, the way you manage e-mail should also evolve. Taking time to evaluate the effectiveness of labels, priorities, and automation rules can help keep the inbox a productive work environment.

Maintaining an organized and tidy inbox is essential for effective management of incoming e-mail. It is a common situation in my experience to have overcrowded inboxes with hundreds or even thousands of messages yet to be read. Such a scenario can be indicative of various problematic aspects in managing digital communications:

1. **Poor Consideration for Received Messages:** A flooded inbox may reflect a tendency to underestimate the importance of reading and managing e-mail. In this case, e-mail review is often postponed until the end of the day, when one is less energetic and focused,

making this activity a marginal task. Not only can this approach lead to delays in responding to important communications, but it also risks conveying a perception of neglect or disinterest in senders.

2. **Multiple Delayed or Not Yet Started Tasks:** An excess of unread e-mails may also signal the presence of numerous outstanding tasks. This excess may be the result of difficulties in managing and prioritizing tasks, or of a workload that exceeds management capacity. The accumulation of unread messages may therefore be symptomatic of a broader time management and prioritization problem that requires immediate attention and more effective management strategies.

3. **Poor Organization of Incoming E-mail:** Finally, an excessive amount of unimportant and non-urgent e-mail left in the inbox can indicate poor organization. Without an effective filtering and categorization system, less relevant e-mails can easily overload the inbox, making it difficult to identify and access urgent or important communications. This can lead to the risk of overlooking or missing crucial messages, with potential negative consequences in terms of job opportunities, missed deadlines, or communication problems.

Any of these three causes, alone or competing with each other, is potentially a symptom of a lack of respect for one's own or others' work; in the case of an accumulation of unread mail due to an excessive workload, the situation may obviously not be the result of a deliberate choice, but rather of external circumstances.

Inbound Emails

However, even in these situations, it is important to recognize the individual's responsibility to manage his or her time and resources optimally. Lack of a proactive strategy to deal with overwork can lead to ineffective e-mail management, with negative consequences for both the individual and the team or organization.

It is a common misconception that one's inbox is a private recess, hidden from the eyes of others. However, in reality, there are many situations in the work environment where our inbox can become visible to others. From the colleague who stands beside our desk to collaborate on a project, to sharing a screen during a video call, the opportunities for others to catch a glimpse of our e-mail are more frequent than we might think.

And while it is true that no one will go into detail to read our e-mails, the number of unread messages in our inbox is a detail that easily jumps out at you.

This seemingly innocuous aspect can actually convey a lot about our professionalism and the way we work. A high number of unread messages could be interpreted as a sign of disorganization or inability to efficiently manage one's workload. This perception could influence how colleagues and superiors view our reliability and professional commitment.

In addition, inbox management can also reflect our approach to communication and collaboration within the group. A neat and well-managed inbox suggests a meticulous and careful approach, qualities valued in any professional environment.

Conversely, a neglected inbox may give the impression of a less serious approach to teamwork and project management.

Therefore, it is important to be aware that, even if unintentionally, our e-mail inbox can become a window through which colleagues and co-workers perceive our work style.

Maintaining orderly and systematic e-mail management not only helps us to be more productive and not lose important information, but also helps to build and maintain a good professional reputation. In an increasingly digitized and interconnected working world, small details such as e-mail management can have a significant impact on our professional image.

Management of Priorities

As we have seen, a professional's inbox, in its incessant daily flow, can turn into a veritable sea of messages, each demanding a specific form of attention, resulting in timely responses, methodical organization, and careful management of priorities.

This reality is as much a challenge as it is an opportunity to demonstrate effectiveness and competence in managing digital communications. In this dynamic environment, the ability to discern between what is urgent and what is important becomes a critical skill.

Each e-mail that arrives in the inbox carries with it its own level of priority, defined by its content, sender, and timing.

Inbound Emails

Some messages may be urgent in nature, requiring an immediate response to resolve critical issues or capitalize on temporary opportunities. Others might be important but not urgent, allowing for more thoughtful planning and thoughtful response.

Properly understanding and assessing the degree of importance and urgency of each message is crucial to ensuring that the most critical issues receive the attention they deserve, while avoiding being swept into a vortex of constant responsiveness to less important emails.

Establishing a hierarchy of priorities in email inbox management is a key strategic move for any professional. Not only does this process focus attention on messages that require immediate action, but it also transforms the entire e-mail management experience into a more structured and controlled activity.

Determining which e-mails need urgent responses and which can be handled later helps optimize the use of time and resources, ensuring that critical tasks receive the attention and promptness they deserve.

In this context, the use of the Eisenhower matrix emerges as an effective tool for e-mail prioritization.

The Eisenhower matrix, named after U.S. President Dwight D. Eisenhower (1890-1969) who inspired it[6] , is a time

---

[6] Dwight D. Eisenhower, in a 1954 speech explained that "I have two kinds

management method based on distinguishing between tasks according to their urgency and importance. The matrix is divided into four quadrants:

1. **Important and Urgent:** These tasks require immediate attention and are usually related to deadlines and crises. In email management, messages from key customers or emails that require a quick response to solve urgent problems fall into this category.

2. **Important but Not Urgent:** These tasks are important for long-term success and require strategic planning. In email management, they may include communications that require thoughtful response or project planning.

3. **Urgent but Not Important:** These tasks take time but do not contribute significantly to long-term goals. In the context of e-mail, they may be requests that can be delegated to others or that require a quick response but are not crucial.

---

of *problems, the urgent and the important. The urgent are not important, and the important are never urgent"* ("I have two kinds of problems, the urgent and the important. The urgent are not important, and the important are never urgent.").

This quote, more than thirty years later, was the basis on which American writer Stephen Covey (1932-2012) in his book "*The Seven Habits of Highly Effective People*" (in Italy "The Seven Pillars of Success," 1991, Bompiani) elaborated what is now known as the "Eisenhower Matrix" (or, more rarely, "Covey's"): a basis for objective analysis of activity prioritization.

Inbound Emails

4. **Neither Important nor Urgent:** These tasks offer the least value and should be eliminated or minimized. Emails that fall into this category may include spam, unsolicited newsletters, or messages that do not require direct action.

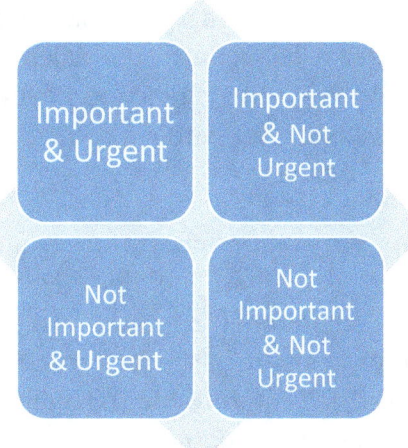

Applying the Eisenhower matrix to e-mail management means evaluating each message received and deciding in which quadrant it fits. This allows you to determine whether to respond immediately, schedule a specific time for a more detailed response, delegate the response to another person, or simply delete or archive the message.

My formula in particular applies rules and subfolders automatically based on the principles of this Matrix:

1. **Important and Urgent:** E-mail is automatically marked as Important if it comes from one of my superiors or operational contacts. These are emails that I read

immediately and assign urgency to if they have a tight deadline: then they are the first actions I take.

2. **Important but Not Urgent:** Emails that are automatically marked as important because they are received from one of my superiors or operational contacts, but have a time-delayed deadline. In this case, I set a deadline in the calendar by blocking a space of time in my agency to devote to this activity by the weekend (or within a couple of days before the indicated deadline)

3. Urgent **but Not Important**: Emails with urgent requests, but where neither my superiors nor the various operational contacts are senders or copy recipients, are usually forwarded directly to the operators dedicated to the specific task, correlated by a small Call To Action in which I ask them to perform checks or activities requested in the forwarded email.

4. **Neither Important nor Urgent:** All e-mails in which my name is exclusively in CC are automatically diverted to a subfolder that I check and "manage" once a week.

The Answers

In the context of message responses, each element of the topic under discussion must be examined to avoid ambiguity or the need for further explanation. This detailed approach is focal to avoid any form of ambiguity or misunderstanding that might otherwise require further communication

Inbound Emails

exchanges to clarify. A well thought out and carefully structured response not only demonstrates professionalism but also respect toward the sender, as it reflects careful consideration of their words and the context of the message.

Clarity in communication, therefore, becomes a key concept. When responding to a message, whether it is a complex request, a status update, or a simple confirmation, the first crucial point is to make sure that you fully understand the content and intent of the communication received.

This may require careful reading and, in some cases, re-reading of the original message to ensure that all nuances and key points are captured. Once this understanding is established, it is essential that the response reflect that understanding so that the recipient can clearly perceive that their message has been fully assimilated and considered.

Clarity in response is especially important when dealing with complex or sensitive issues. In such cases, it may be helpful to briefly summarize the understanding of the message received before providing one's response or point of view. This serves to reassure the sender that their message has been interpreted correctly and establishes a common basis for further discussion.

The tone and style used in responses to e-mail messages, or in any form of written communication, require special attention and careful consideration. How we articulate our responses can have a significant impact on how our message is perceived and, consequently, on the quality of the professional or personal relationship. Maintaining a professional and courteous tone is critical, especially in situations that may be charged with tension or where there is a risk of misunderstanding.

Word choice is crucial: harsh expressions, aggressive tones or offensive language should be avoided at all costs. Even when disagreeing or responding to a message that might seem provocative or confusing, it is important to express your thoughts in a respectful and constructive manner. The use of thoughtful and measured language not only helps keep one calm in a potentially charged conversation, but also demonstrates maturity and professionalism.

For example, a response such as "*I didn't understand a word you wrote*" can be perceived as aggressive and rude, creating a wall between the sender and the recipient. This kind of language can easily exacerbate an already tense situation and lead to fruitless communication or, worse, damage professional relationships. In contrast, a phrase such as "I *don't think I understand what you mean*" is much more effective in communicating a lack of understanding or disagreement. Not only does this approach open the door for further clarification, but it does so in a respectful manner, maintaining an environment of constructive dialogue.

It is also important to consider the context and relationship to the recipient when choosing the tone and style of the response. What is appropriate in a communication with a long-time colleague may not be appropriate with a new client or a superior. Sensitivity to context and the ability to adapt one's communication style to different situations are key skills in effective communication.

Inbound Emails

It is understood that in drafting a response it is necessary to apply all the normal accuracy of writing an e-mail as reviewed above.

Timeliness in communications represents a delicate balance between being responsive and taking the time to provide accurate and well-considered responses. Responding promptly to messages demonstrates a high degree of professionalism and respect for colleagues and their commitments. This is particularly relevant in contexts where timely decisions are crucial or where delays in responses can cause misunderstandings or operational slowdowns.

However, speed should never compromise the quality of communication. Responding too quickly, without taking the time to fully assess the situation or formulate an accurate response, can lead to rushed and potentially misleading communications. Rushed responses can leave questions unanswered or create new ambiguities, which will then require further clarification, increasing the workload and the possibility of errors.

In addition, responding in a thoughtful manner allows one to consider all the implications of a communication and to examine different perspectives before acting. This thoughtful approach not only improves the quality of the response but also conveys a sense of consideration and competence.

Another factor to consider is the nature of the message received. Some communications may require an immediate response, while others may be more complex and require more in-depth analysis. Distinguishing between these two

Inbound Emails

categories and responding accordingly is a key skill in effective communications management.

In some cases, it may be helpful to communicate an initial acknowledgement of the message received, followed by a more detailed response at a later time. This approach demonstrates care and commitment without sacrificing the need for adequate reflection.

Finding a way to estimate the time it takes to provide an accurate response and communicating this quickly to the recipient is my way of resolving the situation:

"Good morning,
I am retrieving the transaction history, I estimate I can send you a complete analysis by tomorrow night."

Inbound Emails

Chapter Summary

Without proper management, the e-mail inbox can quickly become chaotic, making it difficult to distinguish important messages from less relevant ones. Modern e-mail systems offer features such as automated rules that assign specific labels to e-mails based on criteria such as the sender, keywords in the subject line, or message body. This automation helps focus on the most relevant messages without spending too much time on manual organization.

Creating custom categories or labels is an effective way to organize messages into homogeneous groups. It is advisable to study the divisions and titles by which communications are categorized and then consistently apply these labels manually or through automation (such as Outlook rules).

Using search filters for keywords, dates, senders, or attachment sizes can save time otherwise spent scrolling through long chains of messages.

Rather than keeping all messages in the inbox, archiving those that do not require immediate action or have already been processed helps keep the inbox focused on current activities, while less urgent information is still easily accessible for future reference.

In a professional environment, an overloaded inbox can be a sign of poor digital communications management. An excessive number of unread e-mails may indicate a lack of attention to incoming messages, a backlog of tasks, or poor organizational skills. It is essential to recognize individual responsibility in effectively managing one's time and resources.

Discerning between urgent and important e-mails is a crucial skill in managing digital communication. Applying the Eisenhower Matrix can help prioritize e-mails, distinguishing between those that require immediate attention and those that allow for more thoughtful planning and response. Customized rules and folders based on this principle can help manage the e-mail workload efficiently.

Clarity in email responses is essential. Before responding, it is essential to understand the content and intent of the message received. Maintaining a professional and courteous tone, even in disagreements or potentially provocative situations, demonstrates maturity and professionalism. Word choice and sensitivity to context and relationship to the recipient are critical to effective communication.

Organizing Meetings

The Connected World Meetings

As global businesses expand, the use of online meeting tools has become inevitable. However, it is critical to understand that online meetings are not simply a digital version of physical meetings. There are, in fact, significant differences between these two modes that go far beyond mere physical distance.

The most obvious difference is precisely that of physical distance. While in face-to-face meetings people are in the same physical space, in online meetings participants are often located in different parts of the world.

This geographical distance can create special challenges in communication and active participation. For example, nonverbal nuances such as body language or facial expression, which are easily perceived in physical meetings, become almost invisible in an online context.

Also, in physical meetings, it is easier to monitor the activity and engagement of participants simply by observing the room. In online meetings, this information may be less obvious. It can be difficult, for example, to tell if a participant is distracted or working on another project during the meeting. Therefore, it is critical to encourage active participation and ensure that all participants feel involved and heard.

Given these differences, the organization of online meetings becomes a crucial element in their success. A well-organized meeting is more likely to achieve its objectives and engage participants effectively. This means that it is necessary to plan ahead, set a clear agenda, and provide all necessary materials before the meeting.

In addition, using features such as question-and-answer sessions during the meeting can help keep engagement levels high.

Another aspect to consider is time management. Online meetings should be concise and to the point, as attention span can decline more quickly in a virtual environment than in a physical one. It is also helpful to provide short breaks

Organizing Meetings

during longer meetings to avoid screen fatigue and keep energy high among participants.

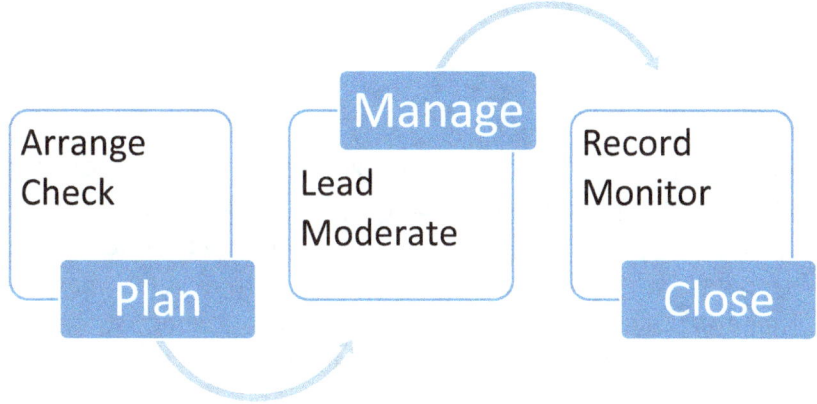

Successful Meetings

Online meetings have become an everyday reality in many business environments, especially with the rise of remote work and digital communication solutions.

But how can we ensure that these meetings are truly useful and effective? The answer lies largely in organization and management.

Without a well-defined structure, meetings can become chaotic, disorganized, and ultimately unproductive. This not only wastes valuable time, but can also lead to frustration and disengagement on the part of participants.

Falling into the mistake of believing that a remote meeting is easy because it is extremely simple to create with a few quick steps can be misleading: every meeting requires a more or less extensive organizational phase.

Tools and Technology

Ensuring that all participants have access to the tools and technology needed to effectively participate in an online meeting is a vital aspect of meeting management in a modern work environment. This not only ensures that the meeting can run smoothly, but also demonstrates a commitment to inclusiveness and efficiency.

Choosing the right videoconferencing platform is the critical first step. It is important to select software that is reliable, easy to use, and accessible for all participants. This may require evaluating the different options available and selecting the one that best fits the team's needs.

The platform should support essential features such as screen sharing, meeting recording, and integrated chat to ensure smooth and comprehensive communication.

In addition to the videoconferencing platform, it is essential to ensure that all participants have access to the necessary documents and resources. This could include agendas, presentations, reports or any other supporting materials that will be used during the meeting.

Using document sharing tools such as Microsoft OneDrive, Google Drive, or Dropbox can facilitate real-time access and collaboration, allowing everyone to be on the same page even if from different computers.

Another important aspect is familiarity with the tools used. If you are not relying on company tools, the knowledge and training of which is the responsibility of the company and individual employees, prior to the meeting, it may be helpful to provide participants with tutorials on how to use the videoconferencing platform and other digital tools.

This helps reduce technology anxiety and ensures that everyone feels comfortable using the necessary technology. It is critical not to assume that any participants from outside our organization are familiar with our business assets: if, for example, the company we work for is fluent in Zoom, it is safe to assume that colleagues know how to use it, but not all the suppliers or customers we may need to invite to the meeting.

In addition, it is useful to consider accessibility needs. This includes making sure that technology is accessible to people with disabilities, such as providing subtitles for the deaf or making sure that materials are readable for those with visual impairments. This is not only a matter of legal compliance, but also a sign of respect and inclusion for all members of the group.

Targeted Netiquette Rules

Establishing ground rules for Netiquette during online meetings is a critical step in ensuring that they are productive and respectful. These rules are not just a set of conventions;

they represent a collective commitment to a collaborative and respectful work environment.

One of the most important rules is to "mute" the microphone (i.e., disable incoming audio) when not speaking. This simple act reduces background noise and accidental interruptions, allowing the speaker to be heard clearly.

All major online meeting software has a button-usually in the shape of the microphone itself-to turn the incoming audio on or off and be able to manage its on or off with a single click.

Another basic rule is to avoid interrupting others. In a virtual environment, where nonverbal signals are limited, it is easy to accidentally overlap during a conversation.

Waiting for someone to finish speaking before intervening is not only a matter of courtesy, but also facilitates smoother and more understandable communication. This mutual respect creates an atmosphere of active listening, where every voice is heard and every opinion is considered.

In addition, it is essential to ensure that everyone has the opportunity to contribute. In a meeting, each participant brings a unique and valuable perspective.

The meeting moderator should actively encourage everyone's participation, especially those who tend to be more reserved. This can be done by asking direct questions or creating dedicated spaces where each participant can express his or her ideas without interruption.

Using tools such as chat during the meeting can also be an effective way to ensure that everyone can contribute.

Those who may not feel comfortable intervening verbally can use chat to share their thoughts. This method ensures that even the quietest voices are heard and that every contribution is considered.

Finally, it is important that these rules of conduct be clearly communicated at the beginning of each meeting and adhered to by all participants. This not only improves the quality of communication, but also reinforces a sense of community and mutual respect within the team.

If, for example, the organizer knows that people with connection problems are attending, it might be appropriate for him to explicitly ask all participants at the beginning of the meeting to turn off their cameras to lighten the amount of data transmitted and facilitate those with weak connectivities.

Time Management

Time management in an online meeting is an art that requires precision and attention. Starting and finishing on time is more than a formality; it is a demonstration of respect for the time of all participants.

This aspect is critical to establishing a professional and productive work environment. When you start on time, you send a clear message: every moment is precious and should be made the most of.

Creating an agenda well structured is the first step toward an effective meeting. Each agenda item should have an allotted time, commensurate with its importance. Not only does this help keep the discussion focused, but it also ensures that all topics are properly addressed.

The moderator's role here becomes crucial; he or she must guide the discussion, making sure that it stays within the allotted time and that each topic gets the attention it deserves.

It is not uncommon for some discussions to extend beyond the scheduled time. In these cases, it is important to have the flexibility to adapt. The moderator may decide to move the discussion to the end of the meeting or, if necessary, to schedule a separate meeting.

This approach ensures that other agenda items are not neglected and that the meeting remains productive.

The use of visible scheduling tools and timers can be a great help in time management. These tools help keep track of the time spent on each topic and keep everyone aware of the schedule. Also, in longer meetings, including scheduled breaks is essential.

These breaks not only provide a time to rest, but can also be an opportunity to reflect on the topics discussed and prepare for the next phase of the discussion.

For participants in an online meeting, Time Management starts with showing up to the meeting on time and ends with self-regulating one's speech so that there is room for everyone.

Special emphasis should be placed on punctuality: online meetings are often such short time windows that even a 5-minute delay can jeopardize success. The famous "academic quarter-hour" considered an acceptable delay by the professor before a lecture begins is not applicable to a 30-minute meeting, the effectiveness of which would be halved.

Meetings are a fundamental part of business life and can have a significant impact on the effectiveness and success of the organization.

Therefore, organizing an effective meeting requires careful planning, setting clear objectives, and selecting the right participants.

Define the Main Objective

Before you start planning a meeting, it is essential to have a clearly defined goal.

The question is, "*What do we want to get out of this meeting?*"

Goals can vary widely, from discussing new ideas to making focal decisions or simply sharing updates. Defining the main goal will give you clear guidance throughout the planning process.

In addition to the main objective, identify the specific goals you wish to achieve during the meeting.

These may include:

- Discussion of specific topics.
- Searching for solutions to problems.
- Decisions on future actions.
- Sharing of key information.

Having specific objectives will help you identify exactly the participants you need and structure the meeting agenda in more detail by including the outline of all topics to be covered.

Defining the Agenda

A well-structured agenda is essential for a successful meeting. Based on your main and specific objectives, create a list of topics to be addressed during the meeting. Assign each topic an approximate time to ensure you stick to the agenda.

The agenda is translated into the so-called "Agenda" (OdG), which is a list of topics scheduled for discussion at the meeting.

The SO is usually drafted as a list so as to clearly divide the various issues, which also become for all intents and purposes visually the "agenda items" during the moderation and conduct of the meeting.

If the meeting is on platforms shared with the workgroup or organization to which we belong, such as on Microsoft Teams, it is an excellent strategy to include the SO directly in the meeting invitation, i.e., in the email that automatically starts to forward the meeting to all invited participants.

This will enable those in attendance to be immediately aware of the topics to be discussed at the meeting.

Select Key Participants

Including only people whose input is essential to achieving the meeting's objectives is vital. This strategic choice serves to keep the meeting focused, avoiding digressions and wasted time.

Selecting participants for a meeting is a key process in ensuring that the meeting is not only productive but also efficient. It is a practice that requires care and consideration, similar to selecting the recipients of an e-mail, where "To" participants represent those who are essential, while those in "Cc" are the optional participants.

"To" (or "Required" in some videoconferencing programs) participants are those who have an active role in the meeting. They are the key stakeholders, those who have decisions to make or crucial information to provide or obtain.

When selecting these participants, ask yourself:

- Do they have a direct role in achieving the goals of the meeting?
- Can they provide indispensable input or make key decisions?
- Would their absence preclude the progress or conclusion of the discussion?
- Is the information that will be shared critical to them?

Participants in "Cc" (or "Optional" in some videoconferencing programs) are those who benefit from being informed but do not have an active or decisive role, whose work activities will not change based on the content or decisions made in the meeting.

They may be people who:

- They will be involved in later stages of the project.
- They request to be updated but without actively participating in the discussion.
- They may offer occasional input or additional perspective.

Establish Date, Time and Duration

The choice of date and time for a meeting is a key element that can determine its success. Finding a balance that satisfies most participants while ensuring that there is sufficient time to cover all topics without rushing is essential. Careful planning of date and time is critical. A meeting scheduled at an inconvenient time can lead to poor attendance or uninvolved participation.

It is essential to consider the time zones of the participants, especially in geographically distributed groups, but even more important is to take into account the standard work schedules and commitments of all invitees so as to identify sufficient time space (or "slot") for discussion without having to rush content.

Another consideration not to forget is to try never to send requests to attend meetings that are exactly consecutive (or preceding) others already scheduled on others' calendars. Allowing participants at least 15 minutes between our proposed meeting and others already on his or her daily schedule is a practice I have always tried to promote.

This 15-minute "space" is both time-sensitive (if the previous meeting needs a few extra minutes, it will not impact the start of our meeting) and time-sensitive for the guests (who will have time to have a glass of water or take stock of our topics instead of having to catapult from one meeting to another).

Video conferencing platforms offer scheduling tools that make it easier to choose dates and times by allowing us to take all these factors into account with minimal effort.

These tools make it possible to:

- View participants' shared agendas to easily identify common windows of time.
- Automatically suggest free time slots, reducing the need for e-mail exchanges to confirm availability.
- Directly manage time change proposals from invitees by integrating them with the monitoring of all participants' agendas.

Microsoft Outlook, for example, with its "Scheduling Assistant" tool allows all these scheduling steps to be managed with a visual interface on the commitments on the calendars of all the recipients of the meeting.

This is why it is a good practice to always keep one's schedule up-to-date: those who need to invite us to a meeting will know when we are free!

Prepare Support Materials

Properly preparing the supporting materials needed for a meeting, such as presentations, documents or reference data, is a key step in ensuring that the meeting is efficient and productive. The key is to ensure that all materials are accessible to all participants, whether they are in physical presence or connected virtually.

Materials should be clear, concise, and relevant to the topics covered in the meeting. Including key information that guides or supports the discussion and structuring them to be easily understood helps participants better orient themselves during the meeting.

Sharing these materials in advance allows participants to consult and understand the information in advance, thus preparing constructive questions, comments or contributions.

This approach contributes significantly to making the meeting more focused and productive, minimizing downtime and maximizing active participation.

The use of cloud sharing platforms such as Google Drive or OneDrive proves extremely useful. These tools offer universal accessibility, allowing participants to access materials from any location and device.

The ability to collaborate in real time on documents enables last-minute preparation or updates, while the version history preserves different versions of documents, ensuring traceability of changes and providing clear context for any alterations made.

Of course, sending via e-mail is still a great alternative, but beware: if sent too far in advance, e-mails may not be properly archived by recipients, who in some cases may not find them nimbly before the meeting, even thwarting prior sending.

For this reason, if instead of quickly accessible shared folders you opt for emailing, always consider that there is the possibility of attaching documents to the meeting invitation itself, either when you create it or by simply updating it and adding the documents as soon as they are ready-that way it will be impossible to miss it quickly!

It is important to remember, in fact, that when sending an invitation to attend a meeting to the various participants, the management programs are literally sending an e-mail containing the information and the link to the online meeting.

This e-mail can then be leveraged to include everything that is needed for the meeting to be a success and for the various participants to have all the preparatory information they may need to prepare for the meeting.

Effective Leadership

Whether informal meetings, team meetings, or brainstorming sessions, meetings can often become a waste of time if not managed effectively.

Productivity in meetings is essential to make the best use of company time and resources. An effective meeting should lead to measurable results and contribute to the achievement of business goals.

It is good to focus on some reasons why productivity in meetings is so crucial:

- Saving Time: Time is precious in a business environment. Prolonged, non-productive meetings can be a great waste of time for all participants.
- Maintaining Commitment: People are more engaged and motivated when they see that a meeting is progressing efficiently and bringing concrete results.
- Respect for Resources: Each participant in a meeting represents a valuable resource to the company. Using their time effectively is a sign of respect for their contribution.
- Improved Decision Making: Productive meetings lead to better, more informed decisions because all participants have the opportunity to contribute meaningfully.

For these optimizations to be effective and efficient, it is essential that meetings are not only carefully organized, but also conducted in a focused and prepared manner.

The meeting organizer is and should also be the moderator and "facilitator" of the meeting.

The Facilitator

A facilitator, in the context of meetings, is a professional figure who specializes in guiding groups of people through processes of discussion, decision-making, or problem-solving. The term "facilitator" is derived from the verb "to facilitate," which means - precisely - that he or she must "make easy" the meeting, and this reflects exactly the key role of this figure: to make easier and more effective, the process of communication and collaboration within a group.

The facilitator focuses on "how" the discussion takes place, rather than on "what" is discussed. His or her function is not to make decisions or bring content input, but to guide the group through a structured path of dialogue and interaction.

One of the key aspects of the facilitator's role is neutrality. The facilitator does not actively participate in the content of the discussion, but maintains an impartial attitude, focusing on assisting the group to achieve its goals.

The facilitator monitors and manages group dynamics. This includes encouraging balanced participation, ensuring that all points of view are heard, and mitigating any conflicts or tensions that arise during discussion.

A key task of the facilitator is to ensure that the meeting proceeds efficiently, staying focused on the predefined objectives and adhering to the established timelines.

Respect the Times

One of the most common challenges encountered during meetings is exceeding the scheduled time. This phenomenon, which is quite common, can reduce the effectiveness of the meeting and negatively affect participant engagement. Strictly adhering to the time allocated to each agenda item is therefore not only a sign of professionalism, but a practical necessity to ensure that all topics receive the attention they deserve.

The meeting organizer, in this context, takes on a key role, that of the "time keeper." This figure is in charge of monitoring the progress of the meeting, making sure that it proceeds according to the established timetable.

To play this role effectively, the time keeper must be attentive and diplomatic, able to gently interrupt digressions or prolonged discussions that may derail the meeting from its goals.

An effective time keeper uses several tools and techniques to keep the meeting on track: it can be helpful to establish clear rules at the beginning of the meeting, communicating openly how time will be managed and what is expected of each participant in terms of contribution and adherence to the agenda.

Another effective approach can be the use of discrete signals or agreed-upon codes to indicate when the time allotted to a topic is about to run out: very common in in-person debates is the use, for example, of two quick, sharp taps on one's microphone by the moderator who is thus alerting the speaker that his or her time is up.

Organizing Meetings

In a remote meeting this may be slightly more complicated, but clear communication at the beginning of the meeting will still allow the facilitator to use channels such as chat linked to the meeting or to politely interrupt the speaker when the set time is exceeded without being offensive.

In addition, the moderator can take responsibility for summarizing the key points of a discussion and suggesting that any further discussion or debate be moved to a later time, perhaps dedicating a specific session to that topic.

It is crucial that the facilitator operates with a balance between firmness and sensitivity, recognizing the importance of each contribution, but also the importance of respecting the time of all participants.

This not only improves meeting efficiency, but also helps create a respectful and productive work environment where each person's time and efforts are valued.

Actively Involve Participants

Active and involved participation of team members not only enriches the discussion with different perspectives, but also helps to keep overall interest high, preventing distraction and passivity.

An effective method to stimulate this type of participation is to ask focused questions. These questions should be open-ended and designed to encourage reflection and debate. For example, asking "*What are your thoughts on this strategy?*" or "*How could we improve this process?*" invites participants to share their opinions and ideas in a constructive way.

Actively asking for participants' opinions is another way to ensure that everyone feels heard and involved. This can be especially important for those who tend to be less vocal in a group setting.

Directing the floor directly to these individuals, or asking for their input on specific topics, can encourage more balanced participation and enrich the discussion with a variety of perspectives.

Actively involving participants in the discussion goes beyond simply asking for feedback. It involves creating an environment in which everyone feels comfortable sharing their ideas and thoughts. This can include structuring the meeting in a way that promotes interaction, such as creating small working groups or using collaborative brainstorming activities.

It is also important to recognize and value the contributions of participants. This not only boosts team members' confidence and self-esteem, but also creates a positive environment that encourages further active participation. A simple "*Thank you for your contribution*" or "*This is a great idea, let's explore it further*" can go a long way in fostering a collaborative and engaging environment.

Use Support Tools

The use of tools such as visual presentations or screen-sharing software is an important resource in meetings, as they can significantly help maintain focus on the discussion. These tools provide visual support that can make concepts clearer and easier to understand, helping participants follow the flow of the conversation and stay focused on the topics being discussed.

However, it is critical to use such tools purposefully to prevent them from becoming a distraction. An effective visual presentation should be clear, concise, and closely related to the agenda topics. It is important to avoid overloading the slides with too much text or complex graphics, which can be counterproductive and divert attention from the main talk.

Screen sharing, if used appropriately, can also be a great way to guide participants through specific documents, show real-time data, or facilitate collaborative workshops and brainstorms.

However, it is essential that the use of these tools is well integrated into the flow of the meeting. Frequent interruptions to solve technical problems or complicated transitions between different screens can interrupt the pace of the discussion and reduce the efficiency of the meeting.

To maximize the effectiveness of these tools, the meeting organizer should familiarize himself or herself with the software in advance and prepare materials for presentation. This includes checking the functionality of the technology before the meeting and making sure that all materials are ready and accessible.

Forward planning can also involve sharing the papers prepared by the other participants with the moderator in advance: that way if any of them had technical problems, the facilitator could take over the "projection" of the papers during the speech of others.

Questions and answers during the meeting

Meetings are a fertile ground for the exchange of ideas and collective problem solving. However, their effectiveness depends heavily on the ability to handle Question & Answer (Q&A) sessions.

These moments are critical to ensure that all participants have a clear understanding of the topics being discussed and that their concerns have been heard and considered. Underestimating this stage can lead to misunderstandings or a lack of communication, with consequences that can extend far beyond the meeting itself.

To optimize the D&R session, it is critical to integrate it strategically within the meeting agenda. Dedicating a specific time at the end of the meeting allows you to focus on the presentations and discussions without interruption, knowing that there will be time set aside to explore doubts and issues in depth.

This approach also helps participants formulate more thoughtful and relevant questions, having had time to digest the information presented.

Early communication of this dedicated space for questions is equally important. Informing participants at the beginning of the meeting of the existence of a D&R segment invites them to note their questions as they arise, ensuring that these questions are not forgotten or overlooked.

To ensure that the process of collecting questions is efficient, especially in meetings with many participants or in virtual meetings, it may be useful to designate a person responsible for this activity.

Using digital tools such as an online meeting chat or a shared document can simplify the collection and organization of questions. In a physical meeting, a simple sheet of paper or a whiteboard can serve the same function. It is essential that the method chosen is clear to everyone and communicated from the outset to avoid confusion and ensure that every question is recorded.

When the time comes to address questions, the meeting facilitator, armed with the list of collected questions, can efficiently guide the D&R session. Answering questions in an orderly and systematic manner ensures that each participant feels heard and that the most relevant questions receive the attention they deserve.

If time is a limiting factor, prioritizing becomes crucial, perhaps prioritizing questions that concern most participants or are most pertinent to the objectives of the meeting.

Concluding the D&R session with a summary is a key step in strengthening collective understanding and ensuring that all participants have a clear understanding of the information exchanged.

This summary can also serve as a starting point for post-meeting follow-up, especially if some questions are left unanswered due to time constraints.

Technical problems?

Whether it's a drop in connection speed in a remote meeting or a whiteboard malfunction in an in-person meeting, the ability to handle technical glitches can make the difference between a productive meeting and a collective loss of time.

The moderator and/or organizer of an online meeting need not be an IT expert, and there is no requirement that there be a technical attendant at every single meeting: while it may be suitable for an event with hundreds of participants to have at least one IT support worker present, it would be unthinkable to have an attendant at every online meeting of an entire organization.

For this reason, there are some tricks that proper planning and preparation can put in place so that the meeting and its participants can deal with technical problems even in the complete absence of a dedicated operator present in real time at the meeting.

Preparation and Prevention

First of all, prevention is key. Making sure that all equipment is in working order before the meeting begins can avoid many problems.

This includes testing the Internet connection, projection devices, audio and video systems, and any other technological tools that will be used.

Having a Plan B for each critical component of the meeting is a good practice: for example, having a mobile hotspot available in case the Wi-Fi connection gives out, or a whiteboard and markers if the interactive whiteboard fails.

During the Meeting

Despite the best preparation, technical problems can always occur. In such cases, it is necessary to remain calm: it is important for the meeting facilitator to remain calm and reassuring.

Tension can easily spread, if only because of the risk of going over schedule; therefore, a quiet presence can help maintain order and manage the situation.

In these situations it is essential, in order:

Communicate: Inform participants that you are aware of the problem and are working to solve it. If the problem cannot be solved quickly, communicate an alternative plan of action.

Assess the impact: Quickly determine how much the technical problem is affecting the meeting. If it is a minor problem, perhaps you can continue while someone works on the solution. If it is a major problem, you may need to take a break or reconvene the meeting.

Switch to plan B: If the problem persists, switch to the alternative plan already arranged. For example, if the video connection is unstable, switch to a conference call.

Use technical support: If available, involve technical support immediately. Having IT support contacts on hand can expedite problem resolution.

Specific Problems and Solutions

Some of the common habits for solving the most common problems during Remote Meetings:

- Drop in connection speed: If the Internet connection becomes unstable, ask participants to turn off webcams to reduce the load on the bandwidth.
- Meetings software that doesn't work: Having alternate links ready on different platforms can save the day. If Zoom doesn't work, switch to Teams or Google Meet, for example.
- Disturbed audio: If audio is problematic, ask everyone to mute their microphones when not speaking. If the problem is with a single user, ask the specific participant to reconnect--wait while attempting to do so--or to continue the discussion via chat or through alternative links, such as telephone.

For "hybrid" meetings that are partly online and partly in-person, the advice is extremely similar:

- Blackboard malfunction: If the interactive whiteboard does not work, switch to a traditional whiteboard. If not available, use a shared whiteboard app on tablets or laptops projected from your computer screen.
- Problems with the projector: Having spare cables and adapters to connect different types of devices can quickly solve the problem. If the projector does not work at all, distribute printed materials and/or share the presentation via e-mail or on a shared platform.

After the Meeting

Once the meeting is over, it is important to do an analysis of the problem to prevent it from happening again in the future. Recording the incident, the actions taken, and the solutions found can be useful for the IT team and for improving the prevention plan.

Also, if the problem had a significant impact on the meeting, consider sending a summary or recording to participants to make sure everyone has the information they need.

Language Barriers

Running a meeting where participants speak different languages presents a significant communication challenge, but also an opportunity to exercise inclusiveness and effectiveness in corporate communication. In a global context, English often emerges as a lingua franca, allowing people of different nationalities to interact on a common platform.

However, the choice of corporate language or English is not just a convention, but a practical necessity that aims to ensure that all participants can follow and contribute to the discussion equally.

The decision to use English or the corporate language as the primary means of communication should be clearly communicated in the meeting invitation and reiterated at the beginning of the meeting. This ensures that everyone is aware of the expectations and can prepare accordingly, for example, by preparing key terms and concepts in advance.

In particularly large meetings or occasions such as online training sessions, it is also important to check for any translation or interpretation needs for those who may not feel comfortable with the main language.

During the meeting, the facilitator is responsible for moderating the conversation, ensuring that the language used is accessible to all. This may involve simplifying language, using slides or supporting visual materials, and asking for clarification or paraphrasing when using technical or industry-specific terms that may not be immediately understandable to everyone.

It is inevitable that, in some cases, small groups of participants who share the same native language may feel more comfortable discussing with each other in that language. While this may facilitate communication and the development of ideas within that group, it is critical that this does not exclude other participants.

Therefore, ground rules need to be established: if you are to speak in a minority language, you must first notify the rest of the group and then provide a summary in the main language or in English.

This summary should not just be a mere translation, but should capture the essence of the discussion, ensuring that key points, decisions, and actions are understood by all.

The summary should be concise and focused, avoiding getting lost in superfluous details that might confuse rather than clarify. In addition, it is important for the facilitator to encourage questions and clarification after each summary to ensure that all participants have the same understanding of the topics covered.

This is especially important when discussing complex concepts or making decisions that require group consensus.

In addition, technology can play a crucial role in supporting communication in a multilingual meeting. Machine translation tools and subtitling software can provide immediate, though not always perfect, support for those who may have difficulty with the main language.

However, it is essential that these tools be used as a support and not as a substitute for active and direct communication between participants.

Finally, it is important for the meeting facilitator to have a good command of the main language and cross-cultural dynamics. This means not only being able to speak the language, but also understanding the cultural nuances and sensitivities that can affect communication.

An effective facilitator is one who can navigate these complexities with empathy and skill, ensuring that all participants feel heard, respected and involved.

Documentation and Actions

Meeting documentation and post-meeting action management are aspects that go far beyond mere bureaucratic formality; in fact, they are fundamental pillars for the success of any organization.

These processes are the real value-add that allows you to capture crucial details, make informed decisions, and plan effective actions. Without accurate recording and judicious management, information is at risk of being dispersed, decisions of being forgotten, and actions of remaining unimplemented.

Let's start with the documentation of meetings. This practice is not only a way to keep track of what was said and decided, but also serves as a historical record that can be consulted in the future to resolve disagreements or clarify obscure points.

Documentation should be as detailed as necessary to provide a complete picture of the meeting. This includes a list of participants, topics discussed, decisions made, and actions assigned. In addition, recording the timelines for each agenda item can provide valuable context.

Another key aspect of documentation is the clarity and accuracy of the language used. Avoiding ambiguity and unclear technical terms is essential to ensure that all team members, regardless of their background or level of experience, can understand the content.

In addition, documentation should be made available to all group members as soon as possible after the meeting to ensure that action can be taken in a timely manner.

The MOM

The Minute of Meeting, or MOM (it is also "Minute of Meeting" in English, so it retains the same acronym), is an essential document that provides a detailed account of the topics discussed, decisions made, and actions to be taken.

This text begins by recording basic information such as the date, time and place of the meeting, as well as a list of present and absent participants.

A detailed summary of the topics discussed follows, usually reflecting the order of the agenda planned for the meeting. Each agenda item is covered separately, providing an accurate account of the discussions, including the various opinions and significant contributions of the participants.

Decisions made during the meeting should be clearly noted down, outlining future actions and specifying who is responsible for each action, along with the corresponding deadlines. This step is crucial for what was "said" to become what was "decided"-only the written form can make clear and foolproof all that transpired in the meeting.

The Minute, incidentally, also includes topics that, although not part of the pre-set agenda, emerge during the meeting and are deemed relevant. This kind of information, if not immediately translated into text, is at very high risk of being forgotten as it is not even on the meeting agenda.

Drafting the Minute requires attention to detail and an iron adherence to objectivity. The person in charge of this drafting is dedicated to faithfully capturing the reality of the meeting without being drawn into personal interpretations. An effective MOM is simple, schematic and extremely "neutral," with short sentences and preferring quick lists to long paragraphs.

Rather than
"Luke will take care of downloading the history of the last three years from the archives and send it to the supplier within a week from today."

is preferable something like
"Three-year history submission to vendor - By the end of the week (by Luca)"

Once completed, the Minute should be distributed among all invitees for final review and approval, ensuring that the document accurately represents what happened during the meeting.

For an online meeting, usually the calendars of e-mail programs allow a message to be sent to all the names involved in the meeting by an automatic function: on Microsoft Outlook, for example, right-clicking on the appointment in the calendar brings up the "Reply to All" function that creates an e-mail message with all the participants already listed in "To" (if mandatory) or "cc" (if optional).

If the meeting hosted a Question and Answer session, it is good practice to include the most relevant ones in the Minute.

I usually keep an e-mail or open text sheet directly during meetings with the agenda on it, so that decisions and actions already broken down by topic are noted in real time.This way, at the end of the meeting I only need a short time to check the form and the Minute is practically ready.

This is, of course, only possible if you are not "sharing the screen" with other participants, or if you are sharing only a particular program and not the whole screen, or if the meeting is informal enough that it is not a problem to let everyone see your notes in progress.

Tracking Tools

In post-meeting management, the use of task management tools plays a key role in simplifying the tracking of actions to be taken, the setting of deadlines, and the optimization of communication among team members. A practical example of how these tools can be used effectively is the use of Microsoft Planner or other similar programs in a business setting.

If our organization routinely uses any method of action tracking, even just a shared "To Do" list or the like, it is up to the meeting organizer not only to draft the Minute, but also to integrate its contents into the programs usually used by the company.

It is useful to remember that even the simple filing of the Minute itself could be a business practice or procedure: knowing the internal rules is the basis for being able to comply fully with them and make the meeting held functional to the specific needs and demands of your company.

Follow-Up and Review

One of the components of the post-meeting could be to schedule a subsequent regular follow-up meeting on the assigned actions. This is not only a way to track progress, but also an opportunity to bring the team together and address any obstacles together. Follow-up meetings thus become not only moments of verification, but also spaces for collective sharing and solution.

To ensure that these new meetings are effective, it is essential that they contain a clear record of the actions decided upon earlier. Here, the importance of using the MOM of previous meetings as a supporting document becomes apparent. The MOM serves as a historical diary of the events, decisions, and actions that were agreed upon, providing context and a solid basis for current discussion.

When organizing a follow-up meeting, reproposing the same agenda from the previous meeting, supplemented with any additions or corrections, helps to maintain a logical and consistent thread. In addition, attaching the previous MOM as early as the invitation phase of the new meeting ensures that all participants have all the information they need to prepare properly.

This approach not only facilitates effective tracking of actions, but also promotes a culture of accountability and transparency. Each team member thus has the opportunity to see how his or her actions contribute to the larger picture and to better understand his or her role in achieving common goals.

Evaluate and Improve

After each meeting, taking time for in-depth reflection is essential not only to evaluate the effectiveness of the meeting itself, but also to refine communication and organizational techniques and strategies for future meetings.

This process of self-analysis and continuous improvement is critical for the meeting organizer, who must set out to ensure that each subsequent meeting is more productive and satisfying than the previous one.

In this evaluation, it is crucial to consider several aspects. First and foremost is the ability to clearly establish the objectives of the meeting and ensure that they have actually been achieved.

It is crucial to ask, "*Did we meet initial expectations? Were the agenda items effectively addressed?*" Reviewing every aspect of the meeting, from member participation and interaction to time management and use of technology tools, offers valuable insights into what worked well and what needs improvement.

Another key aspect is the quality of communication. Reflecting on the dynamics of dialogue and interaction within the meeting can reveal much about how to better facilitate participation and engagement of team members.

Questions such as, "*Did all participants have an opportunity to express themselves? Were there barriers or obstacles to effective communication?*" are essential to understanding and improving the atmosphere and effectiveness of dialogue during meetings.

The organizer should also consider the effectiveness of the tools and techniques used and the effectiveness of post-meeting actions.

Through this process of self-assessment and reflection, the meeting organizer can continue to develop and refine his or her skills, ensuring that each meeting is a step toward increasingly efficient, productive, and satisfying meetings.

Organizing Meetings

Chapter Summary

The use of online meeting tools has become indispensable, marking a marked evolution from traditional physical meetings. These digital platforms, while overcoming the barriers of physical distance, introduce unique challenges in terms of communication and participant engagement. The lack of nonverbal cues, for example, can make it more complex to perceive participants' reactions and engagement, underscoring the importance of targeted strategies to facilitate interaction and ensure that everyone feels included.

It is vital to avoid believing that they are simple to set up just because they are easy to create. Choosing the right videoconferencing platform, ensuring that all participants have access to the necessary tools and technology, and familiarizing themselves with these tools are key steps.

Elements such as advance planning, setting a clear agenda, and distributing necessary materials in advance become essential. Active participation can be encouraged through the use of Q&A sessions, while careful time management is essential to maintain focus and minimize digital fatigue.

A focal aspect is ensuring universal access to the tools and technologies needed to participate effectively in meetings. Selecting a video conferencing platform that is reliable, easy to use, and accessible for all participants is the critical first step. Features such as screen sharing, meeting recording, and integrated chat enrich the experience, facilitating smooth and comprehensive communication.

Netiquette specific to online meetings establishes ground rules for a collaborative and respectful environment. Practices such as disabling audio when not speaking and waiting your turn to speak are essential for smooth and respectful communication. These rules not only improve the quality of communication but also strengthen the sense of community and mutual respect within the team.

Effective time management, organizing a well-structured agenda, and careful selection of participants are key to making online meetings efficient and fruitful.

Crucial is the writing of final documentation for an effective conclusion and confirmation that the communication was a success.

Attending Meetings

Presence in the Connected World

Anyone who finds himself or herself having to attend a business meeting as part of the group of speakers involved should always keep in mind what has already been said about organizing meetings: due preparation is functional to the success of the meeting regardless of its duration.

Preparing slides and necessary documents in advance is essential not only for the organizer but for anyone who is expected to take an active part in a meeting, even if only for a talk. A fortiori, the shorter the contribution, the more preparation is needed to meet the given timeframe.

While it is true that it is the moderator who has to keep track of the time taken by the participants and adherence to the schedule, it is everyone's job to help make this possible: if I had only 5 minutes for my talk, it would be illogical and disrespectful to prepare a 50-slide presentation and perhaps during the meeting demand to show and explain them all.

Many of the tips presented in the chapter on meeting organization are useful not only for moderators but also for participants. For example, although it is the moderator's job to raise awareness about the appropriate use of video cameras, it is essential that each participant demonstrate the same awareness regarding his or her presence at the event, deciding when it is appropriate to turn his or her camera off or on.

It is also important to pay attention to details that are critical for anyone participating in an online meeting. These details are crucial to ensuring that meetings are productive and efficient, despite the physical distances and challenges posed by technological tools. Careful management of these aspects facilitates smoother interactions and more effective execution of the established agenda.

Meetings should always be seen as an intersection between input and output, that is, between information received (input) and information delivered (output).

Viewing each meeting as either a source of input or the need to share an output (or both) is the key to making each meeting an effective working tool.

Pre-Meeting Preparation

Participating effectively in a meeting begins well before it takes place. Proper preparation can make the difference between a productive meeting and one that seems like a waste of time.

First, it is critical to understand the purpose of the meeting. Whether it is a brainstorming session, a decision to be made, or a project update, each type of meeting has a specific purpose. Sometimes the purpose may be clear from the agenda; other times you may need to ask the convener for more details. Knowing the purpose of the meeting will help focus your preparation on the issues that will be most relevant.

Once the goal of the meeting has been defined, the next step becomes research. This involves carefully gathering information relevant to the topic of discussion. For example, if the meeting deals with a technical issue discussed in previous days, it is reasonable to expect participants to spend a few minutes reviewing previous e-mail correspondence. This allows everyone to get a clear view of the current status of the issues under consideration.

Attending Meeting

Preparing in this way is essential to stay in line with the purpose of the meeting and to maximize the efficiency of the time available. Such preparation avoids the need to recapitulate information already known and shared, while respecting other participants' time. Instead of spending the first few minutes of the meeting going over old topics, participants can directly proceed with the discussion on a common basis. This attitude not only shows respect for others' time but also contributes significantly to the effectiveness of the meeting.

Preliminary research allows you to enter the meeting with a well-informed overview, ready to contribute hard data and facts to the discussion. This preparation helps guide the conversation productively, facilitating informed and constructive decision making.

Prepare Questions and Discussion Points

Preparing a list of questions and discussion points is critical to the productivity of a meeting. Such preparation not only manifests interest and engagement, but also allows the flow of conversation to be actively directed toward topics deemed important.

Asking thought-provoking questions or requesting additional information can enrich the discussion considerably. These questions encourage participants to think critically and explore aspects of the problem that may have been overlooked. Similarly, emphasizing key points in the discussion helps to keep the focus of the meeting on the stated objectives.

Formulating thought-provoking questions or soliciting additional information can greatly enrich the discussion. Such questions prompt participants to critically analyze and explore in depth aspects of the problem that may have been overlooked. Similarly, highlighting key points during the discussion helps to keep the focus of the meeting on its intended goals.

It is not strictly necessary to draw up a list of questions or turn it into a presentation; however, one of the best practices is to briefly reflect on personal goals for the meeting. Even if the organizer has convened the meeting with a specific purpose, it is essential that each participant identify and clarify his or her personal interests to maximize his or her contribution.

For example, while the organizer may have called a meeting to select a solution to an operational problem, the goal of an invited technician might be to ensure that all participants understand the impact of each solution on operations. In parallel, a representative of the administrative function might aim to understand the cost of the options discussed, regardless of the final choice.

Every meeting is a dynamic interaction, and it is crucial that each participant maintains a clear understanding of his or her interest in the context of the meeting. This prevents passive and inattentive participation, valuing the time invested in the meeting. Picking up on the previous example, if the administrative representative neglects to express his or her concerns during the meeting, an additional meeting or series of e-mails may be necessary to clarify costs, an activity that could have been effectively handled during the first meeting,

Attending Meeting

maximizing the benefits for all and avoiding unnecessary subsequent time investment.

Verify Technology

A reliable connection is the foundation for smooth and uninterrupted communication, a key element in the success of any online meeting. In addition, it is important to ensure that the video conferencing software being used is not only up to date with the latest versions, but also fully operational. Regular updates often include significant improvements in security and functionality, elements that can directly affect the effectiveness of communication.

Equally critical is familiarity with the chosen software. Knowing how to navigate the various features and use the available tools effectively can significantly reduce the technical time spent on adaptation during the meeting, thereby maximizing the time spent on actual discussion.

Finally, it is essential to check that devices such as microphone and camera are properly configured. Clear audio and a crisp image are crucial to maintain a professional level of communication and to avoid misunderstandings that could arise from poor audiovisual quality.

Implementing these technology audits before each online meeting not only increases the professionalism of participation, but also reduces the risk of technical interruptions that could hinder communication and meeting efficiency. This proactive approach to technology readiness ensures that all parties involved can fully focus on the topics under discussion, optimizing meeting outcomes and respecting each participant's time.

Prepare Supporting Materials

Advance preparation of all supporting materials is essential when planning to present or support topics with data during a meeting. Whether presentations, charts or documents, having these items readily available and easily accessible during the meeting is of paramount importance. This allows for a more persuasive and organized exposition of arguments, ensuring a smooth narrative free of interruptions caused by searching for the necessary materials.

Sharing materials in advance with the organizer or a colleague can greatly improve the effectiveness of the presentation during a meeting. This approach is particularly useful in situations where less familiar or potentially unreliable technologies are expected to be used. A common example involves attending a meeting using a mobile device, such as a cell phone, rather than a traditional computer.

Sending your presentation in advance to another participant can ensure adequate technical support during the meeting. This person can assist in managing the materials, ensuring that the presentation proceeds smoothly, despite the possible limitations imposed by cell phone use.

This not only facilitates the conduct of the intervention, but also helps to maintain a high level of professionalism and fluency of communication: careful preparation of information supports reflects a professional and well-organized approach, which is essential for dealing with discussions effectively.

Virtual Label in Meeting

Virtual etiquette in online meetings is a key aspect that ensures successful video conferences. Proper handling of tools such as the video camera and microphone, combined with respect for virtual manners, helps to create a professional and respectful environment.

First, the use of the video camera should be considered carefully. Turning the camera on when speaking not only demonstrates presence and active participation, but also facilitates nonverbal communication, a key element in human interaction. However, it is important to assess the context and specifics of the meeting to decide when it is appropriate to keep the camera on or off in order to respect the privacy and preferences of all participants.

Microphone management is equally worthy of attention. Keeping the microphone off when not speaking can prevent noise and background noise, which can easily distract other participants and interrupt the flow of discussion. Turning the microphone on only when it is your turn to speak improves audio clarity and communication efficiency.

Virtual manners also include being on time for online appointments, prepared with the necessary materials, and ready to actively participate. It is also important to show respect and consideration for others' contributions, waiting your turn to speak and avoiding distracting behavior. Acknowledging and responding appropriately to the contributions of others not only promotes constructive dialogue, but also strengthens the sense of cooperation and mutual respect within the group.

Adopting these norms of behavior not only elevates the quality of interactions during video conferences, but also sets a standard of professionalism and courtesy that enriches the experience of all participants, making each meeting more productive and enjoyable.

Constructive Interaction

Knowing how to intervene effectively requires a combination of appropriate timing, ability to express disagreement in a respectful manner, and the competence to contribute in a balanced manner without overpowering other participants.

Timeliness (or, in English "timing") is a key element. Intervening at the right time can mean the difference between a contribution that is perceived as helpful and one that is seen as a distraction. It is important to listen actively and recognize the appropriate time to insert oneself into the flow of the conversation. This often involves waiting until the end of a thought or topic, or taking advantage of natural pauses in the discussion to ask questions or add relevant information.

When it comes to expressing disagreement, it is essential to do so respectfully. This involves using language that avoids accusatory or overly assertive tones. Phrases such as "*I would have a different opinion*" or "*We might consider another perspective*" are, for example, effective ways to introduce disagreement without belittling others' ideas. It is also helpful to provide justification or data to support one's point of view, which can help other participants see the situation from different angles.

To contribute effectively to a meeting, it is essential to balance your input with that of others. Even if you have strong expertise or many ideas on a topic, dominating the conversation can stifle the input of others and limit diversity of opinion. Therefore, it is important to be aware of how often you interject and make room for others to express themselves as well. Explicitly inviting quieter participants into the dialogue can enrich the discussion with new perspectives and ideas.

By adopting these techniques for constructive interaction, participants can significantly improve the dynamics and effectiveness of meetings. This not only facilitates a more collaborative and respectful work environment, but also stimulates productivity and collective creativity, which are critical to achieving shared goals.

Active Listening and Participation

Active listening and active participation are crucial components that determine the effectiveness of any meeting. These skills not only improve the quality of interactions, but are critical to building a collaborative and respectful work environment.

Active listening involves more than simply hearing the words of others; it requires a conscious effort to fully understand the messages conveyed, both verbal and nonverbal. This type of listening is manifested through behaviors that confirm to others that they are being heard. It involves maintaining eye contact, nodding, using brief verbal statements such as "I understand" or "interesting," and paraphrasing or summarizing what has been said to confirm that they have understood. These actions not only strengthen communication but also convey respect and appreciation for others' ideas, encouraging a more open and honest dialogue.

Beware, however: listening activity is not "showing that you are listening," but Listening and showing that you are actually listening. There is a fundamental difference between four basic attitudes

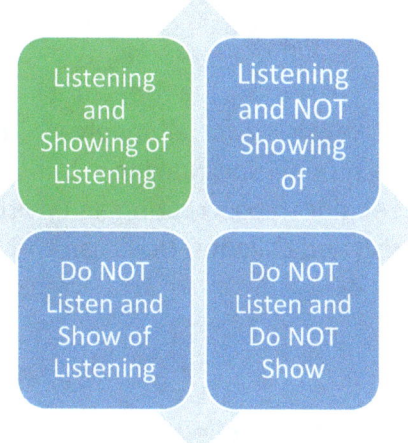

Active listening stands exclusively in the first quadrant, as an added value to effective participation and interest.

Demonstrating engagement through active participation in meetings means contributing meaningfully to the discussion. This may include asking relevant questions, proposing

Attending Meeting

solutions, sharing relevant experiences, or offering constructive feedback. Active participation involves not only talking, but also listening to others and building on their points, connecting ideas and collaborating to deepen the topic at hand.

To facilitate active listening and participation, it is also important to properly manage time and speaking space during meetings. This means making sure that everyone has an opportunity to express themselves and that no dominant voice drowns out the others. It is sometimes helpful to establish ground rules at the beginning of meetings to ensure that all participants are encouraged and able to contribute fairly.

By incorporating active listening and promoting active participation, meetings can become more dynamic, productive, and satisfying for all involved. These approaches not only enrich decision-making, but also strengthen interpersonal relationships, creating an environment in which ideas can flourish and collaborations can thrive.

Post-Meeting Follow-Up

Effective post-meeting follow-up is most important to capitalize on what was discussed during the meeting and to ensure that decisions made lead to concrete results. Follow-up strategies can include summarizing key points, confirming actions to be taken, and ongoing communication with other participants and stakeholders.

While it is true that it is usually the meeting organizer who drafts an accurate MOM, it is not out of the question that one of the participants may offer to do it for him, for example, to allow him to run the meeting without also having to take notes at the same time.

In addition, it is essential to confirm the actions to be taken. This includes sending any emails confirming that they understand the assignment of tasks or responsibilities to specific individuals or teams, with clear deadlines and defined expectations. Ensuring that each action is clearly understood and accepted by those who must execute it is critical to avoid misunderstandings and ensure that progress toward goals is continuous and monitored.

Finally, maintaining open and regular communication with other participants and those interested in the topic at hand is vital. This can include periodic updates on the progress of actions taken, as well as the resolution of any problems that arise during their implementation. Constant communication not only strengthens relationships among group members, but also ensures that everyone remains informed and involved in the process.

By implementing these strategies, post-meeting follow-up becomes an effective extension of the meeting itself, promoting transparency and efficiency. This approach ensures that ideas and decisions made during the meeting are transformed into concrete actions, with a positive impact on the project or the organization as a whole.

Chapter Summary

Effective participation in meetings begins well before the actual meeting, emphasizing the importance of pre-meeting preparation. This process begins with a clear understanding of the purpose of the meeting, which can range from brainstorming to crucial decisions or project updates. Often, objectives are outlined in the agenda, but sometimes they may require direct communication with the organizer for further clarification.

Once the purpose is understood, the stage of gathering relevant information follows, which could include reviewing previous e-mail communications related to the topic under discussion. This preparation allows participants to be aligned and ready to proceed with the discussion on a common basis from the outset, avoiding unnecessary repetition and maximizing the efficiency of their time.

It is also crucial to prepare supporting materials such as presentations, charts, and documents in advance, especially if the time allotted for speaking is limited. An overly long presentation for a short speech is not only disrespectful to others' time but also ineffective.

During the meeting, virtual etiquette requires careful handling of cameras and microphones, as well as behavior that reflects respect and professionalism. Keeping the microphone off when not speaking minimizes distractions, while appropriate use of the camera can enhance nonverbal communication, which is critical for effective human interaction.

In addition, active participation and active listening are essential: contributing relevant questions, offering constructive feedback, and building on the ideas of others not only enriches the discussion but also strengthens the sense of collaboration. It is also important to allow everyone to express themselves fairly, facilitating an inclusive and respectful work environment.

Post-meeting, effective follow-up includes writing and distributing a summary of key points, confirming actions to be taken, and maintaining regular communication with all stakeholders. This ensures that decisions made during the meeting are implemented effectively and that all participants remain updated on the progress of actions taken.

Chat

"A word on the fly?" in digital

In recent years, and particularly in the wake of the 2020 global pandemic, there has been a significant evolution in the use of real-time[7] chat tools in the work environment. The

---

[7] The word "chat," which is derived from the English verb "to *chat" (to* converse informally): the concept of "chat" in online environments began to gain popularity in the 1980s with the arrival of the first online communities and chat rooms ("conversation rooms"). Instant messaging systems such as IRC (Internet Relay Chat), developed by Jarkko Oikarinen in 1988, helped establish and popularize the term "chat" as we know it in the context of online messaging.

pandemic has forced many companies to rapidly shift to remote work, accelerating the adoption of digital communication tools. Real-time chats have become a key means of maintaining daily interactions among team members, compensating for the lack of face-to-face communication.

For companies with multiple domestic and international locations, real-time chats offer a way to connect employees instantly, regardless of time zone or geographic differences. This has enabled greater synchronization and coordination across offices and departments.

Indeed, chat tools allow for a quick and direct exchange of information. Compared to e-mails, which can be more formal and take longer to compose and read, chats offer the possibility of more spontaneous and immediate communication.

Chats have also introduced a more informal tone to professional communication, replacing informal exchanges between colleagues who are in the same room, making the Internet a large collective room. This can facilitate greater openness and smoother communication, especially between closely cooperating colleagues.

These tools offer many advantages in terms of efficiency, speed and flexibility, but they also require careful management to ensure that communication remains effective, professional and secure.

Chat platforms, such as Slack, Microsoft Teams, or even WhatsApp, have revolutionized the way we communicate in

Chat

the work environment. They offer a quick and direct way to share information, collaborate on projects, and maintain connections between geographically distributed teams. However, to use them effectively, it is essential to understand their specific role and functionality.

Effective Use of Chats

Messages should be phrased so that the main point is immediately apparent. This means avoiding the use of slang or technical terminology that may not be familiar to all recipients unless absolutely necessary. Clarity, more than in e-mails, involves the use of simple and direct language, avoiding ambiguities that could lead to misinterpretation or confusion.

Brevity is equally important. Long, rambling messages tend to lose the reader's attention, and should be conveyed via e-mail messages, not chat. The goal should be to communicate the idea or request efficiently, without superfluous detail.

It is always good to remember to maintain a professional tone, avoiding language that is too informal or slangy: using a quick and informal system does not change the fact that it is still a working tool used in a professional context. At the same time, being friendly and approachable to encourage open communication is always recommended for this type of communication.

The Times

Chat

Unlike meetings, which are spaces dedicated to real-time discussion and dialogue, chats offer greater flexibility in response. This feature can be both an advantage and a challenge, as it requires users to balance the need for timely responses with respect for others' time and commitments.

Chats are "asynchronous" communication tools, meaning that they do not require all parties to be available and responsive at the same time. This flexibility allows recipients to respond when it is most appropriate for them, enabling more efficient and less stressful time management.

It is therefore important to set realistic expectations regarding response times in chats. Although the instantaneous nature of chats may suggest the need for an immediate response, it is critical to recognize that colleagues may be engaged in other activities or need time to formulate an appropriate response.

Respecting others' time also means recognizing and understanding their workload and priorities. Pressing for an immediate response can cause unnecessary stress and interfere with their ability to manage their work effectively.

In situations where a quick response is actually needed, it is helpful to clearly communicate the urgency of the message. However, this should be the exception rather than the rule, and used only when absolutely necessary.

Encouraging a culture of mutual respect for each other's time and commitments contributes to a more harmonious and productive work environment. In addition to avoiding

Chat

demanding immediate responses, this includes avoiding texting outside standard working hours or on weekends.

In respecting the timing of others when using chat, it is essential to strike a balance between the need for timely communication and understanding that colleagues have their own schedules and work rhythms. Maintaining this balance is critical to building a collaborative and respectful work environment where digital communication supports, rather than hinders, employee productivity and well-being.

The Tools

Using Groups and Channels

The efficient organization of communication in a digital work environment can be significantly improved through the strategic use of groups and channels based on specific topics. This approach helps keep conversations well organized and makes it easier and faster to retrieve information later.

Creating dedicated groups or channels for different topics or projects allows discussions to be segregated according to their content. For example, separate groups could be created for each project, department or topic of interest within the organization. This allows team members to focus on conversations relevant to their work, reducing information noise from irrelevant discussions.

Another advantage of this thematic organization is the ease of access to information. When conversations are grouped by topic, it becomes easier for group members to trace back to

Chat

specific discussions or shared materials. This is particularly useful in long-term projects or large teams, where the volume of communication can be high and the need to refer back to previous discussions is frequent.

In addition, the use of topic groups or channels can help new team members integrate more easily. They can quickly familiarize themselves with the different topics and projects going on within the organization by reading past conversations in relevant groups.

Managing Notifications

The optimal configuration of notifications is a key aspect of maintaining balance and efficiency in communication within a work environment. Having notification settings that alert the user only to the most important messages is essential to avoid being overwhelmed by an excess of notifications, which can easily become a constant source of distraction.

Chat and notification settings play a crucial role in managing communication and expectations within a work environment. By strategically using chat notification and status settings, you can effectively communicate your availability to others, thus helping to clearly and transparently manage response expectations.

For example, setting a status such as "In meeting" or "Focused on task," sends a clear signal to colleagues that you are momentarily busy and that any response may be delayed. This type of advance communication is extremely useful to avoid misunderstandings or unrealistic expectations regarding the timeliness of responses.

Chat

These status settings provide important flexibility in a dynamic work environment, where team members may find themselves involved in a variety of activities that require different levels of concentration and engagement. For example, a "*Available*" or "*Open to chat*" status may indicate that you are ready and available to interact, while "Do not disturb" may be used for work periods that require high levels of concentration or during important meetings.

In addition, customizing notification settings for specific chats or channels can help reduce information overload, allowing you to focus on the most relevant communications and respond in a more targeted and timely manner.

Integration with Other Work Tools

The integration of chat tools with other platforms used for collaboration and work management is a key step in achieving a higher level of efficiency and optimization of work processes. This technological convergence, which combines instant communication features with project management and collaboration features, transforms chats from simple communication tools to true multifunctional operations centers.

Through the integration, teams can take advantage of the speed and convenience of instant messaging, combining it with the power of project management tools such as document sharing, task scheduling, work progress tracking, and more. This allows team members to access important information, share updates and coordinate effectively, all within a single user-friendly interface.

Chat

The convergence of chat platforms with other work tools facilitates smoother and more organized project management. For example, the ability to quickly turn a chat discussion into a specific action or task without having to leave the messaging platform helps to reduce time consumption and improve the clarity of communication. In addition, by integrating chat with calendars and scheduling, teams can organize meetings and deadlines more easily by automatically synchronizing information across multiple platforms.

This integration makes chat not only a rapid information exchange point, but also a hub for overall task and resource management. The ability to access and manipulate project data directly from chat eliminates the need to constantly switch between platforms, greatly improving productivity and reducing the possibility of errors or omissions.

Sharing Documents

Modern chat tools, which have evolved far beyond their original function as simple messaging platforms, now offer advanced integrations with cloud storage systems and document sharing platforms. This technological synergy radically transforms the way teams work and collaborate by facilitating rapid sharing and access to important files and documents directly through chat. This functionality not only improves the speed and efficiency with which information is distributed within the group, but also greatly increases the accessibility of business-critical data.

With the integration of cloud storage systems into chat platforms, team members can easily upload, share and access

Chat

documents without the need to exit chat or switch to another application. This streamlined workflow means that documents can be quickly passed from one person to another, enabling real-time collaboration and the ability to make informed decisions faster.

In addition, instant access to shared files through chat eliminates many of the traditional steps associated with sharing documents, such as sending attachments via e-mail or the need to log into different systems to retrieve necessary information. Instead, documents can be viewed and edited collaboratively and in real time, allowing team members to make updates, provide feedback or perform revisions efficiently.

This integration of chat, cloud storage, and document sharing platforms not only facilitates collaboration, but also helps keep files and documents organized. With cloud storage, documents are stored securely and centrally, reducing the risk of data loss and simplifying document version management.

Organization of Meetings

The functionality to schedule and organize meetings directly through chat platforms has revolutionized the way meetings are scheduled in the modern business environment. With the introduction of advanced features, such as integration with digital calendars and the ability to send automatic reminders, these chat platforms are no longer just tools for instant messaging, but also become powerful assistants in time and appointment management.

Through integration with digital calendars, users can view the availability of colleagues in real time, making it easier to choose convenient times for all participants. This integration eliminates the need to exchange multiple e-mails or messages to agree on a suitable time, significantly reducing the time spent on meeting planning.

In addition, the ability to set automatic reminders directly through the chat platform ensures that all participants are informed of the upcoming meeting in a timely manner. These reminders can be customized to be sent at specific times before the meeting, ensuring that participants have sufficient time to prepare and reducing the likelihood of missed or delayed attendance.

The use of chat platforms for meeting management also leads to greater organization and preparation. Participants can easily access the agenda, reference materials and other relevant information shared through chat prior to the meeting. This ensures that all participants arrive at the meeting well informed and ready to contribute meaningfully to the discussion.

Project Management

The integration of chat platforms with project management tools represents a significant breakthrough in project planning and tracking. This synergy allows teams to track the progress of activities, assign specific tasks and set deadlines, all within a single, intuitive interface. This type of integration brings with it a number of benefits that improve overall project management.

Chat

A key benefit is the ability to have a clear and up-to-date overview of project status. In a work environment where transparency and accessibility of information are key, this integration allows all team members to quickly view the status of tasks, upcoming deadlines and assigned responsibilities.

Task management becomes more fluid and dynamic with this integration. Team members can receive task assignments directly through chat, with clearly defined details and deadlines. In addition, they can easily report progress or any problems, promoting continuous dialogue and timely resolution of issues.

Collaboration and delegation of tasks within the team are also facilitated by this integration. Team members can collaborate in real time, sharing ideas, feedback and updates on task status. This stimulates a cooperative work environment where information is shared freely and decisions can be made quickly and in an informed manner.

Centralization of Communications

The integration of these different tools into a single chat platform means that teams can access everything they need to work efficiently without having to switch between applications. Project-related information, including communications, documents, appointments and project-specific details, are all grouped together in one easily accessible place. This eliminates the need to search for information through multiple sources, saving time and reducing the possibility of losing crucial information.

Chat

Another significant benefit of this integration is the simplification of workflows. Instead of having to manage multiple applications to communicate, share files or schedule meetings, all of this can be done within the chat platform. Not only does this make processes more streamlined and less error-prone, but it also improves team collaboration, enabling faster and more direct sharing of information.

In addition, having all relevant information and work tools in one place also makes it easier to organize and monitor work. Teams can have a clear view of deadlines, priorities and responsibilities, contributing to a more organized and productive work environment.

Improving Traceability and Accountability.

In a work environment where decisions can be rapid and multiple, having an accessible and organized record of conversations is essential. With chats integrated into broader platforms, every exchange of ideas, every suggestion or agreement is recorded chronologically and easily searchable. This allows team members to return to specific conversations to clarify concerns, verify details or reaffirm agreed goals.

This traceability has a direct and positive impact on project management. Instead of relying on scattered e-mails or scattered notes, teams can refer to a clear and comprehensive chronology of discussions, ensuring that everyone is on the same page regarding goals and commitments. This reduces misunderstandings and improves consistency and efficiency in project progress.

Chat

In addition, the ability to easily track conversations and decisions within the chat platform helps to strengthen accountability within the team. When it is clear who said what and what decisions were made, it is easier for all team members to take responsibility for their actions and contributions.

Optimizing Communication

Establishing clear guidelines on how and when to use chat tools in the work setting is an essential step in maximizing efficiency and maintaining effective communication within the team. Establishing specific rules about what types of communications are best handled through chat and which ones require the use of e-mail or calling a meeting instead helps create an organized and productive work environment.

These guidelines may include guidelines on various aspects of chat communication, such as the relevance of topics to be addressed, appropriate tone and language, and timing for responses. For example, it could be stipulated that chat be used for urgent matters or brief questions that require immediate responses, while more formal or complex communications, such as detailed project proposals or in-depth feedback, should be addressed via e-mail.

Clearly defining which communication medium is most appropriate for each type of message helps reduce ambiguity and ensure that important information is not lost or misinterpreted. For example, establishing that final decisions or important changes to projects should be communicated in a meeting or by e-mail, rather than by chat, ensures that such

Chat

communications receive the appropriate attention and consideration.

In addition, having clear guidelines helps prevent abuse or misuse of chat tools, which can become distracting and reduce productivity. Rules can also help establish clear boundaries between work and private life, preventing easy access to chat from resulting in unrealistic expectations of constant availability.

Archiving functions allow conversations to be preserved, making them accessible even after a period of time. This means that exchanges of information, decisions made and files shared remain available and searchable, without the risk of being lost or forgotten. Such organized archiving contributes to the creation of a digital reference archive, useful for reviewing previous discussions, clarifying any doubts or retrieving relevant information for current or future projects.

The search function, found in most chat platforms, is a powerful tool for quickly locating specific messages, files or discussion topics. Instead of having to manually scroll through long chat histories, users can simply enter keywords or phrases to find exactly what they need. This saves valuable time and makes the process of finding information much more efficient.

These features become especially useful in large teams or complex projects where the volume of communications can be high. Being able to easily store and search information ensures that nothing is lost and that important decisions and discussions can be easily found and used for future decisions or strategies.

In a dynamic work environment, where communication takes place through a variety of channels, it is important to recognize when a topic becomes too complex or sensitive to be adequately handled in a chat room. In such cases, it is advisable to switch to a more direct and personal form of communication, such as a phone call or video conference.

Chat rooms, while useful for quick exchanges of information or brief discussions, may not be ideal for topics that require in-depth discussion or more nuanced communication. This may include situations where detailed elucidations are needed, discussions on sensitive topics, important negotiations, or when misunderstandings or conflicts need to be addressed.

A telephone call or video conference offers many advantages in these situations. First and foremost, verbal communication allows for greater clarity and immediacy. The human voice, and in the case of videoconferencing, body language and facial expressions, can convey emotional and intentional nuances that are difficult to capture in written communication. This helps reduce the risk of misunderstanding and ensure that all parties involved have a clear understanding of the discussion.

In addition, a telephone or video conversation allows for real-time response and interaction, which can be crucial for quickly resolving complex or sensitive issues. The ability to ask questions and receive answers immediately, as well as to discuss and negotiate in real time, makes these forms of

Chat

communication particularly suitable for dealing with topics that require special attention.

In conclusion, while chat is a useful and efficient communication tool, it is important to recognize its limitations and opt for phone calls or video conferencing when topics become too complex or sensitive. This flexibility in the choice of communication channel is critical to maintaining effective communication and a productive work environment.

The emoji

An emoji is a small graphic symbol or icon used to express an emotion, idea or concept nonverbally in digital communications. Derived from the Japanese words "e" (picture) and "moji" (character), the emoji has become a key part of communication in text messages, emails and social media, providing a quick and universal way to express feelings or reactions.

Emoji range from simple yellow faces representing different emotions to a wide range of symbols depicting objects, animals, food, places, activities, and more. Their popularity exploded in the 2010s with the widespread adoption of smartphones, which integrated emoji keyboards.

The use of emoji and gifs[8] in business communications, particularly in chat platforms, can be an effective way to add

Chat

emotional tone and context to messages (the Paraverbal elements). These visual elements can help clarify the intent behind the words, reducing the risk of misunderstandings that can arise in written communication. However, it is critical to use emoji and gifs discreetly and always with the professional context in mind.

In a work environment, emoji and gifs can be used to lighten the tone of a conversation, show approval, solidarity or simply to make a message more friendly and approachable. They can also be useful to express quick reactions or to acknowledge receipt of a message without having to type a full response.

However, it is important to be aware of the context and tone of the conversation and corporate culture. In some situations or work environments, excessive or inappropriate use of emoji and gifs could be perceived as unprofessional or inappropriate. For example, in formal communications, meetings with clients, or situations where serious topics are discussed, the use of these graphic elements may not be appropriate.

In addition, it is important to consider the different cultural interpretations of emoji and to be sensitive to the fact that what may be perceived as friendly or harmless in one culture

---

[8] A GIF, which stands for Graphics Interchange Format, is an image file format that supports both static images and a series of images that create an animated effect.

Chat

may have different connotations in another. This is especially relevant in diverse and multicultural work teams.

The risks of corporate chats

The intensive use of chat platforms in the work environment, while an efficient means of immediate communication, can lead to an overload of messages and notifications. This condition, if not managed properly, can turn into a source of constant distraction or, worse, stress. Therefore, it is essential to develop and adopt effective strategies to manage this information flow so that it remains a useful work tool and does not become a hindrance to productivity.

One of the first strategies may be to set up custom filters and notifications. Users can configure their chat platforms to receive notifications for only the most relevant or urgent messages, thereby reducing the ongoing interruption caused by nonessential notifications. This can include muting notifications from less critical groups or configuring alerts only for direct mentions or specific keywords.

Another useful tactic is to establish specific periods during the day to check and respond to chat messages. This approach, known as "batch processing[9] " of messages, allows

---

[9] Batch processing began in the 1950s and 1960s with the advent of the first computers. At this time, computers were large machines that took up entire rooms, and their use was very expensive and limited to specific business or scientific applications. Computing resources were so limited

Chat

you to focus on tasks without interruption while maintaining regular communication with the group.

In addition, it is important to promote a work culture that recognizes the value of uninterrupted concentration time. This may include encouraging team members to observe "quiet hours" or to use the "*Do Not Disturb*" status when working on tasks that require high concentration.

An additional strategy is training and educating team members on the effective use of chat tools. This includes understanding when it is more appropriate to send an e-mail rather than a chat message, how to formulate clear and concise messages, and how to properly use chat tools to organize and archive conversations.

n an increasingly globalized work environment, where teams and projects can span multiple cultures and countries, it becomes crucial to be sensitive to various corporate cultures and individual communication preferences. This sensitivity is especially important in an international context, where

---

and valuable that they had to be optimized for maximum effect.

Early operating systems designed for these computers, such as the famous IBM 704, used batch processing as the primary method of managing and processing tasks. Users prepared their tasks and data on punch cards or magnetic tapes and sent them to the computer center to be processed in a single group or "batch." This method was efficient for the time because it maximized computer usage by performing a large volume of work at one time.

Chat

cultural differences can significantly influence communication styles and expectations.

Recognizing and respecting different business cultures means understanding that what may be considered normal or acceptable in one culture may not be so in another. For example, the tone of communication, use of formality, expectations of quick response, and even the use of emoji or informal language can vary greatly from one culture to another. Being aware of these differences can help prevent misunderstandings and build stronger, more respectful working relationships.

Likewise, it is important to recognize and adapt to individual communication preferences. Not all team members may feel comfortable with the same communication style or channel. For example, some may prefer more direct communications through calls or video conferences, while others may opt for e-mail or chat messages to allow more time to formulate their responses.

In an international context, it is also critical to be sensitive to language challenges. Although English is often the lingua franca in global business contexts, not everyone may be as fluent or comfortable using a nonnative language. Being patient and encouraging an environment where everyone feels free to express themselves, even if not perfectly, is essential for inclusive and effective communication.

Ensuring that chat communications are secure and compliant with privacy and data protection regulations is of paramount importance. This takes on added importance when it comes

Chat

to sharing sensitive or confidential information through these platforms.

The security of chat communications is about protecting the data exchanged from unauthorized access, interception or loss. It is essential that chat platforms used by businesses implement robust security measures, such as end-to-end encryption, to ensure that conversations and data shared remain private and accessible only to authorized individuals.

In addition, complying with privacy and data protection regulations is crucial to avoid legal penalties and to maintain the trust of customers and employees. This includes adherence to regulations such as the GDPR[10] (General Data Protection Regulation) in the European Union and other privacy laws globally. Companies must ensure that the chat platforms they use are in line with these regulations, especially when it comes to collecting, storing and sharing personal or sensitive data.

To effectively manage the sharing of sensitive or confidential information, companies should also implement clear internal

---

10 The General Data Protection Regulation (GDPR), which came into effect on May 25, 2018, is European Union legislation aimed at strengthening and unifying the protection of personal data of individuals within the EU. The GDPR imposes strict rules on how personal data should be collected, processed and stored, giving individuals more control over their data. The GDPR applies to all organizations, both inside and outside the EU, that process data of EU citizens, introducing heavy penalties for violations.

Chat

policies. These policies should outline what types of information can be shared via chat and what should be communicated through more secure channels. Training employees on best practices for secure information sharing is equally important to reduce the risk of data leaks or privacy breaches.

Awareness of the absence of nonverbal cues in digital communications, particularly chat rooms, is essential to avoid misunderstandings and misinterpretations. In face-to-face communication, a large part of the message is conveyed through body language, facial expressions and tone of voice. When communicating through chat, these nonverbal signals are missing, which can make it more difficult to correctly interpret the intent and tone of the message.

In the absence of these signals, a comment or joke that might be clearly understood as joking or ironic in a face-to-face conversation might be misinterpreted as serious or offensive in a chat room. Similarly, a hastily written message without much detail could be perceived as aloof or cold, even if the intent was neutral or positive.

To mitigate the risk of misunderstandings, it is important to take a clear and direct approach to chat communication. This includes the use of clear, unambiguous language and, where appropriate, the use of emoji to add emotional tone or clarify the intent of a message. However, as mentioned earlier, the use of emoji must be balanced and appropriate to the context.

In addition, it is always best to ask for clarification when in doubt. If a message is unclear or if there is a suspicion that it

Chat

may have been misunderstood, a quick request for clarification can prevent misunderstandings from escalating. This not only helps maintain effective communication, but also helps build a work environment based on clarity and mutual respect.

With the increase in remote work and flexible schedules, the line between time devoted to work and time set aside for private life can easily become blurred. This overlap can lead to a feeling of being "connected" to work all the time, increasing stress and reducing needed time for rest and detachment.

To prevent work chat from encroaching on the personal, it is critical to define and adhere to specific times during which it is appropriate to send work messages. This may include establishing standard work times when you are available for chats and meetings, and times when you are "offline" or unavailable for work communications.

Using status settings and notifications can help communicate these boundaries. For example, setting status to "Do Not Disturb" or "Out of Office" outside work hours can signal to colleagues that you are unavailable. In addition, disabling work chat notifications outside work hours can help prevent the temptation to continually check messages.

It is also important that these boundaries are respected by both employees and superiors. The work culture should encourage respect for personal time and recognize the importance of work-life balance. Leaders and managers should set an example by avoiding sending communications

Chat

outside of agreed-upon hours unless it is for urgent situations.

Chats in the work environment offer immense opportunities to improve communication and collaboration. However, to take full advantage of their benefits requires a balanced approach that takes into account clarity, efficiency, and mutual respect. By integrating these practices into daily routines, chats can become a powerful tool for a more connected and productive work environment.

Chat

Chapter Summary

Real-time chats offer numerous benefits, including the ability to immediately connect employees regardless of geographic or time zone differences. This facilitates greater synchronization and coordination between different offices and departments. Unlike e-mails, which can be more formal and take longer to draft and read, chats allow for more spontaneous and immediate communication.

This form of communication has also introduced a more informal tone to professional interactions, replacing the informal conversations that normally take place between colleagues in the same room. This can foster greater openness and fluidity in communication, especially among those who work closely together. However, managing these tools requires care to ensure that communication remains effective, professional and safe.

Using chat effectively means formulating messages that make the main point immediately clear, avoiding jargon or terminology that is too technical unless strictly necessary. Brevity is crucial: long, rambling messages can lose the reader's attention and are better suited to email. It is also important to maintain a professional tone, despite the informal and fast-paced nature of chat tools.

Chats offer great flexibility in response, which can be both an advantage and a challenge. They do not require the simultaneous availability and responsiveness of the parties, allowing recipients to respond at a time most convenient for them. This can improve time management efficiency and

Chat

reduce stress. However, it is essential to set realistic expectations regarding response times and to respect the timing of others, avoiding pressing for immediate responses that can cause unnecessary stress and interfere with others' ability to manage their own work.

In addition, communication organization can be improved through the strategic use of thematic groups and channels, which help keep conversations organized and simplify information retrieval. Notification management is key to maintaining balance and efficiency by configuring notifications to receive only the most important messages and reducing ongoing interruption caused by nonessential notifications.

Integrating chat platforms with other work tools, such as document sharing, task planning, and project management, can transform chats from simple communication tools to multifunctional operational centers. This enables more effective collaboration and smoother project management, ensuring that decisions and information are quickly shared and accessible within a single user-friendly interface.

Security of communications is of paramount importance, with the need to protect data exchanged from unauthorized access and to comply with privacy and data protection regulations. It is also essential to be aware of the limitations of chat, recognizing when it is more appropriate to use other means of communication, such as phone calls or video conferencing, to deal with topics too complex or sensitive for a chat.

Chat

Conclusion

Etiquette and the Digital World

The digital age has radically transformed the landscape of professional communication. Netiquette in e-mail and meeting management has proven to be not only an essential skill but a true art form.

Each of us, regardless of our work and professional activities, finds ourselves walking the paths of digital communication, having to face the challenge and awareness of how written words and virtual interactions can be honed to forge a respectful, efficient and productive work environment.

Fundamental to always reflect on the ethics of digital communication, touching on issues such as privacy, respect and responsibility, remembering that behind every screen are individuals with their own expectations, needs and limitations.

In conclusion, this is not a technical manual, but an invitation to think about the use of technology to connect people. It is a reminder that despite physical distance, professionalism and the ability to connect should never be underestimated.

These pages provide the tools I have collected over the years to confidently and competently address some of the day-to-day aspects of the Digital Etiquette of Business Communication, with the hope that e-mails will be clear, meetings productive and communication an example of professionalism and personality.

The Author

Born in Livorno, on Tuscany coast, in 1981 and currently living in the metropolitan city of Florence, Italy, *Debora Dini* began her professional career in the Tuscan capital in 2005.

His career has evolved in the field of Outsourcing since 2014 and specifically in Business Process Outsourcing (BPO) since 2019.

His professional experience is distinguished by an approach focused on innovation, continuous improvement, and the strategic use of technology.

Through her work, Debora demonstrates-or seeks to demonstrate-how effective and respectful digital communication can play a key role in the contemporary professional world regardless of the role held or the activities performed.

"*Etiquette of the Connected World*" is his first book, released in Italian in the first edition in 2023 on the Amazon.it platform as an independent publication and evolved in 2024 into the present second edition, the first one in English.